Also by Rich Landau and Kate Jacoby

VEDGE

HORIZONS: NEW VEGAN CUISINE

HORIZONS: THE COOKBOOK

V / STREET

100 Globe-Hopping Plates on the
Cutting Edge of Vegetable Cooking

RICH LANDAU AND KATE JACOBY

WM
WILLIAM MORROW
An Imprint of HarperCollinsPublishers

HarperCollins books may be purchased for educational, business, or sales promotional use. For information please e-mail the Special Markets Department at SPsales@harpercollins.com.

FIRST EDITION

Designed by Ashley Tucker
Photography by Yoni Nimrod
"Travel Journal" photographs by Shutterstock, Inc.

Library of Congress Cataloging-in-Publication Data has been applied for.

ISBN 978-0-06-243848-5

16 17 18 19 20   RRD   10 9 8 7 6 5 4 3 2

BE GOOD.
DO GOOD.
EAT GOOD.

CONTENTS

Introduction 1
Shopping the Markets 5

STICKS 12

SNACKS 28

SALADS & SLAWS 50

MARKET 68

PLATES 92

BOWLS 122

SWEETS 140

COCKTAILS 174

SAUCES, SPICE BLENDS & MARINADES 198

Final Note 213
Universal Conversion Chart 216
Acknowledgments 217
Index 220

INTRODUCTION

One of our favorite questions we ask each other is, "What will be the next big food trend?" We aren't alone in this curiosity—you see it tackled in top food magazines around New Year's when everyone's predicting what will be the hottest ingredient or latest fad. Think kale and sriracha or smoking and pickling. But on a more personal level, we like to test our own culinary inspirations, asking ourselves, "What's next for us?"

After a few years of gorgeous plates served in sophisticated dining rooms, between sips of age-worthy natural wine and intricate Dirt List items on our restaurant Vedge's ever-changing vegetable-driven menus, we felt a little tugging inside. The edgy vegetable restaurant we had opened took on a life of its own, one where we showcase our skills and creativity with elegant compositions and careful pairings, poised service and polished hospitality. The little tugging grew stronger. Vedge has become a serious dining experience where we challenge ourselves to jump new culinary hurdles and set new standards for vegetable cooking. We began to feel a need to express the other side of our culinary spirit.

What about the fiery dan dan sauce and kung pao? How could we introduce za'atar and harissa? Could we get away with a fried tempeh taco at happy hour or an ais kacang for dessert? So when we asked ourselves what's next in restaurants and what's next for us, we found ourselves drawn to street food. We were booking flights to Hong Kong, choosing hotels near night markets in Munich, passing on the fancy restaurants in the Caribbean in favor of the taxi drivers' favorite lunch spots. We love a good white tablecloth, but the excitement wasn't being served on china. We found ourselves drawn to lawn furniture and picnic benches, little stands and shacks with smoke billowing out the roof, and sand floors and dirt floors, where you can pick up the food with your bare hands, douse it with hot sauce, and wash it all down with a cold beer sipped right from the bottle. It was a natural progression for us, and it's what gave way to V Street.

This is our new playground, a street food bar where we draw inspiration from some of the greatest culinary traditions all over the world. Yes, we still highlight vegetables, putting their flavors and textures front and center in every dish, but we draw our inspiration from iconic dishes that define everyday foods across the globe, celebrating cultures from Southeast Asia to Northern Europe, from the Middle East to South America.

There will always be a place for fine dining, a little pampering and celebration. But the dining evolution toward quick and casual goes hand in hand with our insatiable appetite to learn more about the world around us. The world is just a screen away, but we still crave the authentic experience of eating the food. What better way to get to know a new place, its people, and its traditions? We love to travel because we love to expand our culinary experience, and we're most energized these days not by the stuff people learned in gourmet kitchens with a big brigade; we want the stuff that a little older lady is frying up in her sundress and flip flops; the messy, saucy sandwich that guy is eating from a foil wrapper; and whatever is twirling around in that big bowl with chili peppers and fresh herbs chopped up on top—yeah, we'll definitely have what he's having!

So here's a glance into what has been making us tick over the past few years, a collection of recipes we've experimented with, run as specials, and run on our menus since we opened in the fall of 2014. The journeys will continue and the menus will evolve, but the spirit remains the same. Happy travels!

SHOPPING THE MARKETS

Shopping in ethnic markets at home or abroad is a favorite pastime of ours. But even for seasoned travelers and restaurateurs, it can be a little intimidating at times. These days, you can find so much online, and mainstream markets are increasingly reaching out to broader audiences with new ingredients and product lines. But you want to feel like you can hang and be the *cheffy* chef who struts into obscure markets and knows what's up, right?

Well, we can't flip a switch and make that happen for everyone, but we *can* prep you with a few tips that will help. Remember, the recipes in this book are inspired by humble dishes from rich food traditions all over the world where the emphasis is on feeding people a quick meal—not impressing someone in culinary school or a fancy dining room. Learning about a different culture through food is a beautiful thing, and we've been fortunate to find many ethnic markets Stateside that reflect the experiences we seek out when we travel. So capture that spirit, and be just as respectful in the market as if you are visiting the country itself.

Many of our recipes will take well to some substitutions and experimentation. These simple go-to shopping lists cover several ethnic markets, and if you use these as a springboard, you'll have a nicely stocked pantry to get you through much of this book. Good luck!

THE MARKET: INDIAN

As chefs, we are never so uncomfortably out of our element as when in an Indian market. The spices alone are mind-boggling. And when you consider that any self-respecting Indian chef blends all curries from scratch for each and every dish, it's even more humbling. But play around just a little bit. Learning to appreciate each spice both individually and when paired together is a fun culinary exercise; this is a great place to start.

THE BASKET

Basmati rice

Cardamom pods (cook in your basmati rice, then remove)

Fenugreek (critical in curry blends and excellent "secret mystery spice" ingredient)

Garam masala blend (great warming spice)

Papadums, dry or pre-fried

Poha rice

Tamarind paste

Turmeric (fresh)

Yellow lentils

THE MARKET: MEXICAN

Props to the Mexican markets here in Philadelphia—our city has a strong Mexican population, and it shows. Just take a walk through the Italian Market—the same one Rocky made famous in his training montages—and you'll find at least one Latin market stall for every Italian shop. The shop owners are always so friendly, and they play the best music. And we can never resist all the great serving pieces (we have more salsa dishes than we care to admit).

THE BASKET

Adobo spice blend

Black beans

Chipotle (paste or powder)

Habanero hot sauce

Pickled jalapeños

Posole

Refried beans (make sure they're *vegetarian!*)

Tortillas (fresh, 6-inch, wheat and/or corn)

Tortillas (fresh, large, wheat)

Valentina hot sauce

THE MARKET: KOREAN

The Korean markets we've visited are some of the most impressive; the huge Korean population here in Philadelphia obviously demands it. Go to an H Mart and you'll feel as if you just touched down in Seoul. In addition to great Korean items, you'll find lots of Chinese, Japanese, and Vietnamese offerings as well as some lovely homewares if you want to up your service game. (We blow through chopsticks in our house!) H Marts are also great because of their fabulous food courts—it's never fun to shop on an empty stomach, right? So run upstairs and order some *dolsot bibimbap*, then go back to your shopping!

THE BASKET

Bamboo shoots

Daikon

Enoki mushrooms

Five-spice tofu

Gochujang

Kimchi (check the ingredients to make sure it's vegetarian!)

Korean chile flakes (gochugaru)

Korean green radish

Mung bean sprouts

Ssamjang (like gochujang but seasoned with sesame, garlic, and scallions)

THE MARKET: JAPANESE

Japanese markets seem harder to come by here on the East Coast. At present, there's just one in the Philadelphia area. Depending on where you live, you might be better off sourcing Japanese ingredients online or at broader pan-Asian markets.

THE BASKET

Kombu

Mirin rice wine

Miso paste

Nori

Pickled ginger

Rice wine vinegar

Sesame oil

Shiitake mushrooms (dried)

Soba noodles

Sushi rice

Tamari

Tofu (silken and firm)

Togarashi

Udon noodles (fresh)

THE MARKET: **VIETNAMESE AND THAI**

Here's where the fun really starts for us. This is where things get spicy and you get to make all of those crazy red stews and noodles you see on Travel Channel food shows. The flavors here are strong, as are the spices. Always remember to start small—a little goes a long way with a lot of this stuff.

THE BASKET

Chile oil

Coconut milk

Curry paste, green and red (check ingredients to find vegetarian ones)

Jasmine rice

Kaffir lime leaves

Lemongrass (fresh or frozen)

Peanut oil

Pho spice packets (vegetarian)

Pickled chiles

Rice noodles (fresh or dried)

Rice paper wrappers

Sambal oelek

Sriracha

THE MARKET: **CARIBBEAN**

The sweet, spicy flavors of the East Indies converge here. They include influences from Africa, Latin America, and India all coming together to make one big pot of delicious, tropical stew. If you have ever traveled off the beaten path on a Caribbean vacation and found the real food beyond the tourist clichés of mango chutney and pineapple salsa, you'll be right at home here.

THE BASKET

Allspice

Calabaza

Caribbean curry powder from Trinidad or Jamaica

Chayote (also called *cho cho* or *christophine* in the West Indies)

Coconut milk

Jerk sauce (wet)

Jerk spice (dry)

Nutmeg

Red beans

Scotch bonnet hot sauce

THE MARKET: MIDDLE EASTERN

Middle Eastern food, especially Israeli food, is having a moment right now. Though great markets specializing in these foods are currently few and far between, that number will grow more and more quickly as people discover this healthy, light, and flavorful cuisine.

THE BASKET

Bulgur wheat	Paprika	Sesame seeds (white)
Chickpeas	Pita	Sumac (for za'atar)
Cumin	Pomegranates	Tahini
Nigella seeds	Red chiles (for harissa)	Turnips (for pickling)
Olives		

THE BASICS

Here are the top twenty ingredients we use in the book, and why.

Black vinegar: One of the foundations of true Chinese cooking, it's flavored with dried fruit that yields a mysterious subtle sweetness.

Chickpea flour: A staple of Mediterranean cooking, it's gluten-free and unlike most flours it has a great flavor of its own.

Coconut milk: In desserts, this is one of our favorite ingredients for any recipe calling for milk or cream. And because of its rich flavor, it's a perfect addition to many Southeast Asian and Caribbean sauces and stews.

Cumin: Although most people associate cumin with Latin American cooking, it's used all over Asia and the Middle East. When used in restraint, its nutty, earthy, and distinctive flavor can add a new level of depth to savory cooking.

Curry powder: There are more curry powders out there than you could ever try in your lifetime. One mistake people make is not cooking their curry powder in fat. Get it into sizzling oil early to unlock all its personality.

Dijon mustard: Used throughout the world, mustard adds tangy richness and body to sauces: we find Dijon to be the most balanced and versatile.

Five-spice powder: Whether it's the classic Chinese or Vietnamese version, this spice blend adds a whole new dimension of aromatics to your stocks and sauces. Just remember, a little goes a long way, so practice restraint!

Gochugaru: Koreans are very specific about their chiles, and once you try a good Korean chile flake, you'll know why. It's not just heat—it's character. Find the one you like best, and never look back.

Kombu: For a strong shot of umami, you can't beat this seaweed in your soups, stocks, and Asian sauces. There's nothing quite like it. Once you make our dashi with kombu, you'll wonder how you ever lived without it.

Molasses: This dark, sticky syrup is a by-product of the cane sugar-making process. It's absolutely essential for building rich flavor and body in barbecue and jerk.

Rice wine vinegar: An Asian staple, this is made from fermented rice and has a mild acidity that pairs well with any Asian cuisine.

Sambal oelek: Our favorite chile paste, this is a chunky, spicy Southeast Asian condiment. Unlike sriracha, its coarse texture sets it apart.

Sesame oil: The foundation of all good Asian cooking, start your blazing-hot pan off with a touch of sesame oil, and you will be blown away by the flavor it imparts. Always buy toasted sesame oil, and for a deeper, darker touch, buy black sesame oil.

Sherry vinegar: Our favorite vinegar, it's rich and carries a balanced acidity for roasting vegetables and making perfect vinaigrettes. It's proof positive that a nice shot of acidity can wake up flavors without the use of too much salt.

Sriracha: The new ketchup! It's the perfect amount of heat and it's strong on flavor. It can thicken up a broth into a red spicy soup, and it takes any dip, dressing, or spread over the top.

Sunflower oil: Our choice for neutral cooking oil, it holds up to high heat and it's not that expensive.

Tamari: Also known as Japanese soy sauce, a great tamari is like a fine Scotch—full of depth and character. Here is one case where you always want to spend some money for the real deal—no $1.99 bottles of black salt water!

Vegan butter: We love Earth Balance brand to add a nice, luxurious touch of decadence in certain sauces. It also works beautifully as a 1:1 substitution in pastry recipes that call for traditional butter. Park this in your fridge with the vegan mayo, and you're set!

Vegan mayo: Whether you make your own or buy it, vegan mayo is a cornerstone to good cooking. We like Follow Your Heart's Vegenaise best because it's made like a traditional mayonnaise—just using soy in place of eggs. Once you try it, you'll realize there's no reason to eat egg-based mayonnaise again.

White pepper: Sure, this is special because it leaves no flecks behind, but white pepper is its own spice altogether, leaving a fragrant signature on dishes of any ethnicity.

STICKS

Israeli Grilled Eggplant 14

**Palmito with
Malagueta Pepper Sauce** 15

Piri Piri Tofu 17

Tandoor Zucchini 19

Jerk Trumpet Mushrooms 20

Char Siu Tempeh 22

Hoisin-Glazed Seitan Skewers 23

Shishito Robatayaki 25

Chòu Dòufu 26

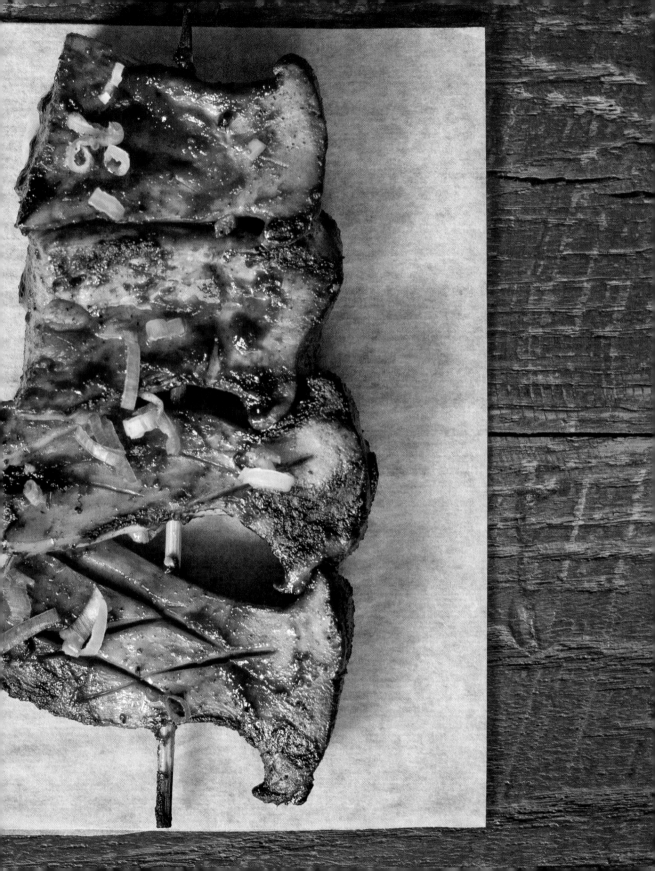

With lots more to offer the world beyond the traditional Middle Eastern repertoire of hummus and pita, Israeli food is very on trend these days. Here's a great way to reimagine the classic baba ghanoush—capturing the true spirit of the region with the aromatic spice blend za'atar, but also encouraging you to fire up your grill and celebrate the texture of a perfectly seared eggplant. **SERVES 4**

ISRAELI GRILLED EGGPLANT

¼ cup sunflower oil

2 tablespoons ketchup

1 teaspoon sherry vinegar

1 garlic clove

1 teaspoon sea salt

2 teaspoons Za'atar (page 208)

2 medium Chinese eggplant, tops trimmed, and sliced in half

1 If using bamboo skewers (as opposed to metal) soak them in water for at least 30 minutes before grilling.

2 Combine the oil, ketchup, vinegar, garlic, and salt in a blender. Blend until smooth, then transfer to a small bowl and whisk in the za'atar.

3 Score the flesh of the eggplant in a hash mark pattern, then slice each half into 3-inch lengths.

4 Using the pre-soaked skewers, slide about 3 pieces of eggplant onto each skewer, spaced about ½ inch apart so they will be easy to handle.

5 Arrange the eggplant skewers on a sheet pan, then brush with the marinade and let sit for at least 15 minutes and up to 1 hour at room temperature.

6 When ready to cook, preheat a chargrill on high or a grill pan over high heat. If you don't have a grill, preheat the oven to broil. Sear the eggplant on both sides until you see nice char marks and crispy edges, 2 to 3 minutes. If using the oven, broil the skewers for 4 to 6 minutes, flipping halfway through to ensure both sides are evenly seared.

Brazilian cuisine is still relatively mysterious here in America. Exotic and hard-to-pronounce dishes like feijoada and moqueca may seem unapproachable, or the recipes are laden with hard-to-source ingredients such as palm oil or açaí. But Brazilian food deserves a special place in world cuisine as its uniqueness defies comparison.

Our most memorable food moment on a trip to Brazil took place in a jaw-dropping outdoor restaurant space etched into the hillside neighborhood of Santa Teresa in Rio. There, we feasted on giant fresh hearts of palm, fileted tableside and served with a simple herb oil. Underneath a canopy of tangled floral vines that danced their way through ancient treetops, we sipped a local pink wine and dipped toasty cassava rolls in just a bit of malagueta pepper sauce. It was divine. This recipe is a little kick-start to bring home some Brazil. **SERVES 4**

PALMITO WITH MALAGUETA PEPPER SAUCE

3 tablespoons sunflower oil

1 tablespoon Latin Spice Blend (page 210)

1 tablespoon malagueta pepper sauce (substitute equal parts Tabasco and sriracha)

1 teaspoon minced garlic

2 teaspoons oregano

2 teaspoons Worcestershire sauce

One 16-ounce can whole hearts of palm (palmito)

1 If using bamboo skewers (as opposed to metal) soak them in water for at least 30 minutes before grilling.

2 Whisk together the oil, Latin Spice Blend, pepper sauce, garlic, oregano, and Worcestershire sauce in a medium bowl until smooth.

3 Cut each palmito stick into three 1½-inch plugs then toss them in the marinade and let them sit for at least 30 minutes and up to 24 hours.

4 Preheat a chargrill to high or a grill pan over high heat and skewer the plugs of palmito, 3 to 5 per stick.

5 Grill the skewers for 3 minutes or until you achieve nice char marks, flipping and rotating once. Serve immediately or chill until ready to serve.

We've had Piri Piri Tofu on our menu, in one form or another, since we opened. The peppers themselves have such great, sharp flavor that they're the perfect source of heat for a bright and tangy sauce. While the three-step baking, marinating, and grilling method might seem a bit obsessive, it is essential for setting the texture of the tofu and locking in flavor. The end result is addictive and can be enjoyed hot or cold, in a taco, or with rice; or be like a chef and just eat it right out of the fridge. You're going to want to keep a lot of these around. **SERVES 4**

PIRI PIRI TOFU

One 16-ounce block
    extra-firm tofu

1 tablespoon tamari

¼ cup sunflower oil

½ cup Piri Piri Marinade
    (page 207)

1 If using bamboo skewers (as opposed to metal) soak them in water for at least 30 minutes before grilling.

2 Preheat the oven to 500°F. Cut the tofu into 4 rectangular planks.

3 Whisk together the tamari and oil in a small bowl. Coat the tofu evenly with the marinade then arrange on a sheet pan with ¼-inch spaces between pieces. Bake for 6 minutes before removing from the oven. Set the tofu aside on the pan for 15 minutes, until tofu is cool enough to handle, then slice into 1-inch cubes.

4 Skewer the tofu cubes onto the pre-soaked skewers, then brush with the piri piri marinade and allow to marinate in the refrigerator for anywhere from 20 minutes to 24 hours—the longer the better.

5 When ready to cook, remove the tofu from the refrigerator. Heat a chargrill to high while the tofu comes up to room temperature (a grill pan will work as well). Sear the tofu skewers, flipping once, until you get nice crisping and charring on all sides, about 4 minutes total. Serve immediately or chill until ready to eat.

At V Street, we're obsessed with freshness, and we always work with the best-quality vegetables we can find. Zucchini is a great example. If you have old, tired, limp zucchini, it will be bitter and flabby. But if you start with beautiful, ripe zucchini with bright, unblemished skin, it will bead a bit of water when you slice through it; that's when you know it's super fresh! Zucchini also happens to be a very versatile vegetable and shows up in many different cuisines from Moroccan to Korean, French to Mexican. Grilled with this marinade, it showcases the flavors of Indian tandoor cooking. While you may not have a tandoor oven in your kitchen, you can mimic the effect by char-blasting the spices on a really hot grill. **SERVES 4 TO 6**

TANDOOR ZUCCHINI

2 medium zucchini

2 teaspoons minced garlic

1 tablespoon chopped scallions (white parts only)

1 teaspoon smoked paprika

1 teaspoon cumin

1 teaspoon thyme

½ cup sunflower oil

1 tablespoon sherry vinegar

½ teaspoon sea salt

½ teaspoon freshly ground black pepper

2 teaspoons curry powder

1 teaspoon tomato paste

1 If using bamboo skewers (as opposed to metal) soak them in water for at least 30 minutes before grilling.

2 Slice the zucchini into ½-inch wheels.

3 Make the marinade by combining the remaining ingredients with 1 tablespoon of water in a blender, and blend until smooth.

4 Arrange the zucchini wheels in a bowl and evenly coat with a thin layer of marinade. Let marinate for at least 15 minutes.

5 When ready to cook, preheat a chargrill on high or a grill pan over high heat. If you don't have a grill, preheat the oven to broil. Using the pre-soaked skewers, slide 3 or 4 marinated wheels onto each skewer, lengthwise. Sear the zucchini on both sides until they develop nice char marks and crispy edges, 2 to 3 minutes. If using the oven, broil the skewers for 4 to 6 minutes, flipping halfway through to ensure both sides are seared evenly.

With just a little heat from Scotch bonnet peppers, jerk sauce is a gorgeous balance between sweet, aromatic spices and tangy, savory notes. Trumpet mushrooms take especially well to this preparation because they're rich and meaty. They grill up beautifully and make the perfect platform for the slightly sticky sauce. **SERVES 4**

JERK TRUMPET MUSHROOMS

12 trumpet mushrooms
(about ¾ pound)

⅓ cup Jerk Sauce (page 206)

1 If using bamboo skewers, soak them in water at least a half hour before using. Metal skewers work just as well.

2 Score the flesh of the mushrooms in a hash mark pattern, then slice each mushroom in half.

3 Coat the mushrooms evenly with the jerk sauce then skewer them onto the pre-soaked skewers.

4 Preheat a chargrill on medium or a grill pan over medium heat. If you don't have a grill, set the oven to broil. Place the skewers on the grill and wait for defined grill marks to develop on the mushrooms and for the marinade to caramelize and yield a dark, rich color on the mushrooms, 3 to 4 minutes. Flip and sear on the other side, 2 to 3 additional minutes. If preparing in the oven, broil the mushrooms for 5 to 7 minutes, turning halfway through. Serve immediately or chill until ready to serve.

Cantonese in origin, char siu is a unique, dark barbecue sauce that has been adopted by many different Asian cultures. Black vinegar is the star here. Tangy, sweet, and unlike anything else, it gives this sauce the complex character that sets it apart from some other, more one-dimensional sweet Asian sauces. Char siu is most often used on protein and served over rice. This method also works great with seitan and tofu; in fact, we love it with tofu on top of Singapore Noodles (page 128). In this dish, char siu, lacquered on slices of baked tempeh, gives it a delicious sweet spicy shine. **SERVES 2 TO 3**

CHAR SIU TEMPEH

1 tablespoon black vinegar

2 tablespoons ketchup

1 tablespoon sriracha

½ tablespoon minced ginger

½ tablespoon minced garlic

2 tablespoons sesame oil

¼ teaspoon five-spice powder

1 tablespoon light brown sugar

3 tablespoons tamari

One 8-ounce package of tempeh

1 Preheat the oven to 400°F. Whisk together all the ingredients, except the tempeh, in a medium bowl until smooth.

2 Slice the tempeh into about 1-inch strips widthwise. Coat the tempeh strips evenly with the char siu sauce then transfer to a sheet pan and roast for 10 to 12 minutes. Alternatively, skewer the tempeh on soaked bamboo skewers and grill on a chargrill over medium heat for 4 to 8 minutes, for extra flavor and to provide an extra-crispy texture.

We avoided hoisin sauce for years, brushing it off as a sticky/sweet mess, a sloppy misrepresentation of an otherwise rich and complex Chinese food culture. We dug a little deeper and uncovered a dark, deep mysterious sauce that tingles with chile, fermented black beans, and black vinegar. Ours is light on sugar and heavy on flavor. We like seitan for this sauce, but try using it on tofu, eggplant, or mushrooms if you'd like. As versatile as they come, this is a great party appetizer but to make it a complete meal, serve it over the Hong Kong Chopped Salad (page 60). **MAKES 8 TO 10 STICKS**

HOISIN-GLAZED SEITAN SKEWERS

HOISIN SAUCE

½ cup rice wine vinegar

½ cup black vinegar

¾ cup tamari

½ cup mirin

¼ cup fermented black bean paste

1 tablespoon sriracha

¼ cup sesame oil

12 to 16 ounces seitan, cut into cubes

2 red bell peppers, cut into 1-inch chunks

12 to 16 scallions (white parts only), cut into 2-inch pieces

1 If using bamboo skewers (as opposed to metal), soak them in water for at least 30 minutes before grilling.

2 Combine all of the hoisin sauce ingredients in a medium saucepan. Bring to a simmer over medium-high heat, then reduce to medium low and cook until the sauce is reduced by half, 8 to 10 minutes. Remove from heat and set aside to cool.

3 Preheat a chargrill to medium-high or preheat the oven to broil.

4 Toss the seitan and vegetables in the hoisin sauce.

5 Alternate the seitan and vegetables on each skewer.

6 Grill the skewers for 2 to 4 minutes on each side or until you see defined char marks and the sauce starts to caramelize. If using a broiler, place the skewers on a sheet pan in the middle of the oven, at least 8 inches away from the flame. Broil for 5 to 8 minutes or until the sauce caramelizes and the seitan darkens.

While the Spanish have tapas bars, the Japanese have izakayas, bustling little gastropubs that serve lots of interesting small-plate examples of some of Japan's best cooking. A quintessential part of many izakayas is a good robatayaki—a chargrill where skewers of all kinds of things are slow-roasted over bincho-tan oak charcoal. In this recipe, we're working with beautiful Japanese peppers that are best when quickly seared, leaving them smoky and grilled on one side and raw and crunchy on the other. If you can't fire up the grill, searing the peppers in a super-hot skillet will also do the trick. **SERVES 6**

SHISHITO ROBATAYAKI

½ cup sesame oil

3 tablespoons tamari

3 tablespoons Togarashi (page 201)

24 shishito peppers

1 Whisk together the sesame oil, tamari, and togarashi in a small bowl.

2 Preheat a chargrill to high or a skillet over high heat. While the grill is heating, soak 6 bamboo skewers in water for 5 minutes.

3 Skewer 4 peppers onto each bamboo skewer, then brush the skewers evenly with the marinade. Grill the peppers on one side just until charred evenly, about 1 minute. Serve immediately.

Introducing stinky tofu. Chòu dòufu is the Chinese method for fermenting then frying tofu, and it definitely lands on the list of acquired tastes. The intensity of the tofu depends on the type of kimchi you use and how long you let it sit and do its thing. If you're new to the concept, start with just twenty-four hours, then try to work your way up to weeklong ferments. Having tried the real thing in Southeast Asia, we can assure you that the real thing is certainly not for everyone. So we recommend using our kimchi, which has a mild quick-ferment. **SERVES 6 TO 8**

CHÒU DÒUFU

Two 16-ounce blocks firm tofu, cut into 2-inch cubes

4 cups kimchi liquid plus 1 cup kimchi (page 85)

Canola oil for frying

1 Arrange the tofu cubes in a large, sterilized, sealable container, layering with some of the kimchi as you go. Then pour the liquid over the tofu to completely submerge it.

2 Seal the container and allow it to sit at room temperature in a cool, dark location (as you would with any pickle) for at least 48 hours.

3 Heat ½ inch of the oil in a large skillet over high heat. Meanwhile, remove the stinky tofu cubes from the container, letting as much liquid drain as possible. You can save the kimchi for soup or another preparation.

4 Fry the tofu cubes until golden brown, about 2 minutes. Remove from the skillet and place on a paper towel–lined plate to remove excess oil. Skewer and serve with more kimchi and hot sauce.

TRAVEL JOURNAL
A MALAGUETA IS A PIRI PIRI

The almost mythical Portuguese islands of Madeira and the Azores seemed a million miles away. But we trekked there in 2012 to find breathtaking beauty and an interesting cuisine hinting of Spanish, African, and French influence—but strangest and greatest of all were these spicy little piri piri peppers. We didn't know it at the time, but for the next few years we would be following Portugal all over the planet.

Macau, we were told, was a Chinese/Portuguese settlement. This we had to see. You arrive to see towering new casinos along the shoreline but it's not until you get back into the old city that you find the soul of Macau. How the Portuguese got all the way across the continent so long ago to this place is mind-boggling.

Here we found Portugal everywhere from the blue-and-white ceramic tiles to the strange mix of Chinese and traditional Portuguese food. It was strange to drink Portuguese Sagres beers so deep in Asia.

Street food was everywhere. We found an amazing peanut butter waffle from a cart that actually made its way onto the V Street dessert menu.

A year later in Brazil, again, we found it fascinating that the tiny country of Portugal managed to get down to South America and colonize this massive territory. We feasted on a fresh hearts of palm salad tingling with lime, cilantro, and chiles; a rich black bean stew; and delicious bread with Portugese olive oil. Malagueta hot sauce on the side seemed familiar, but new.

That evening in Rio the sun was just starting to set as we walked across the street to the beach from the Copacabana Palace. Guitarists were strumming bossa nova and kids were playing soccer on the sand, the air was sweet and thick with sea salt. We settled into café chairs along the promenade and sipped caipirinhas and munched crunchy Globo and papas fritas, with, of course, malagueta hot sauce, and then it dawned on me. A malagueta *is* a piri piri. Nice to know that when Portugal set out to conquer they didn't forget their hot sauce.

SNACKS

5:00 Szechuan Soft Pretzels 30

Chermoula Hummus
with House Pita 32

Fried Pickles
with Spicy Ketchup 34

Potato Pakora
with Tamarind Sauce 36

Scallion Pancakes
with Citrus Ponzu 38

Papadums with Whipped Dal 41

Turnip Cakes
with Honshimeji XO 42

Salchipapas 44

Jerk-Spiced Cashews 46

Sriracha Peanuts 48

Say what you will about cheesesteaks, soft pretzels really do make it into the diet of just about every Philadelphian on a semi-regular basis. We knew they would make a perfect addition to our happy hour scene. Playing off pretzel salt, we decided to amp ours up with a little Szechuan pepper and take things in a fun Chinese direction. Szechuan peppercorns have a nice kick just like fresh black pepper, but they have a floral side to them too—they're aromatic, and they leave a slightly numbing little tingle on your tongue. We pull these out of the oven each day that they're on the menu at 5:00—right on the dot like clockwork, so they're hot and fresh for happy hour! **SERVES 8**

5:00 SZECHUAN SOFT PRETZELS

2 teaspoons sugar

2 teaspoons active dry yeast

1½ cups all-purpose flour plus more for dusting

½ teaspoon sea salt

¾ teaspoon crushed Szechuan peppercorns (substitute equal parts red chile flakes and pink peppercorns)

3 tablespoons vegan butter, melted

¼ cup baking soda

½ teaspoon black lava salt (substitute coarse salt)

Ginger Mustard (page 202), optional

1 Line a sheet pan with parchment paper and set aside. Combine ½ cup warm water, the sugar, and the yeast in a medium bowl and let bloom until the yeast fully activates, about 10 minutes.

2 Sift together the flour, sea salt, and ½ teaspoon of the Szechuan peppercorns in a large bowl. Add the yeast mixture and 1 tablespoon of the melted butter and knead into a dough ball. Set aside in a lightly greased bowl and cover with a clean dish towel to proof in a warm place until the dough has doubled in size, about 45 minutes.

3 Transfer the dough to a lightly floured work surface and cut into 8 equal pieces. Use a rolling pin to roll each dough ball into a 1-inch-thick oval. Place the ovals on the prepared baking sheet and set aside.

4 Preheat the oven to 450°F. Fill a large pot with 8 cups water and bring to a boil over high heat. Slowly add the baking soda a little at a time until fully dissolved. Boil the dough ovals a few at a time, until they rise to the surface of the water, about 30 seconds. Transfer back to the sheet pan.

5 Fold the ovals in half lengthwise to create an Asian-style bun, almost like a thick soft taco, then brush with the remaining melted butter and sprinkle with the remaining Szechuan peppercorns and the lava salt. Bake until golden brown, about 6 minutes. Allow to cool slightly before serving. Take them over the top with Ginger Mustard.

Hummus is one of the most universally loved foods; it's everyone's friend. Here we add a little North African inspiration to the classic Middle Eastern hummus to keep everyone on their toes. Chermoula itself is a marinade based on paprika, ginger, preserved lemon, and cilantro and used throughout parts of Northern Africa. The combination of fresh herbs and intense spices plays really well against the traditional textures of a tahini-rich hummus. **SERVES 4**

CHERMOULA HUMMUS WITH HOUSE PITA

1½ cups cooked chickpeas

⅓ cup olive oil

½ teaspoon sea salt

1 teaspoon freshly ground black pepper

½ teaspoon cumin

⅛ teaspoon smoked paprika, optional

2 teaspoons minced garlic

½ teaspoon minced ginger

¼ cup tahini

2 tablespoons lemon juice

1 teaspoon chopped preserved lemon

¼ cup cilantro, chopped

2 tablespoons chopped parsley

2 tablespoons chopped scallions

1 Soak the chickpeas in ½ cup hot water for 5 minutes to soften. Transfer to a food processor with all the remaining ingredients and process until the mixture is smooth and creamy, about 2 minutes.

2 Transfer to an airtight container and store in the refrigerator for up to 3 days.

3 Serve with warm House Pita (below).

HOUSE PITA

2 tablespoons active dry yeast

¼ cup sugar

8 cups all-purpose flour

¼ cup vegetable oil

1½ tablespoons kosher salt

1 Line two baking sheets with parchment paper and set aside. Combine the yeast and sugar in a large bowl with 3 cups warm water. Allow to bloom for 5 minutes. Then add the flour and oil, first mixing with a spoon then using your hands to create a soft dough ball.

2 Add the kosher salt and continue kneading the dough for 8 minutes or until it forms a clean dough ball that is firm but still sticky. If you prefer to use an electric mixer, use a J-shaped dough hook and knead for 5 minutes, until the dough ball pulls away from the sides of the bowl.

3 Transfer the dough ball to a lightly greased bowl and cover with a clean dish towel, then set aside in a warm place to proof for 1 hour, until doubled in size.

4 Preheat the oven to 450°F. Divide the dough into 20 equal-size portions, each about the size of a large golf ball. An easy way to do this is to cut the dough into 2 equal portions and then 10 equal portions each. Let rest for at least 20 minutes, then flatten into thin disks, about 4 to 5 inches in diameter. Make them as thin as possible. When ready to bake, place on the prepared baking sheets, about 2 inches apart.

5 Place a small, oven-safe dish with ½ cup water in the bottom of the oven to create some steam, then bake the pitas for 6 to 7 minutes, until they start to turn golden brown and puff up about 1 inch in the centers. Best served warm.

MAKES 20 PITA

Southern food is finally coming into its well-deserved spotlight. With a long vegetable growing season, regional spices and grains, and passionate cooks who pay tribute to a rich culinary history while staying in tune with today's trends, the southern food movement seems to have it all. Fried pickles are a southern staple. It may sound strange to us Yankees, but just try one and you'll be hooked on these sour, crunchy, and salty bites. This is a wonderful base recipe for any pickle brine, and we took a few creative liberties with the addition of gochugaru chile flakes to give it a spicy Korean kick. **SERVES 4 TO 6**

FRIED PICKLES WITH SPICY KETCHUP

2½ cups white vinegar

¼ cup sugar

3 tablespoons plus 1 teaspoon salt

5 whole allspice

1 teaspoon gochugaru (Korean chile flakes)

½ teaspoon cumin seeds

½ teaspoon caraway seeds

1 long hot pepper (such as jalapeño), stem removed and sliced in rings

4 cucumbers, sliced into ½-inch wheels

1¾ cups rice flour

2 teaspoons white pepper

1 cup unsweetened soy milk

½ cup Dijon mustard

½ teaspoon freshly ground black pepper

1 tablespoon Togarashi (page 201)

1 Combine ¼ cup water, the vinegar, sugar, 3 tablespoons of the salt, and allspice in a large saucepan. Bring to a boil, then remove from the heat and add the gochugaru, cumin, caraway, and pepper rings.

2 Arrange the cucumber wheels in a sterilized airtight container, then pour the warm brine on top until the vegetables are fully submerged. Seal and store in a cool, dark place for at least 24 and up to 48 hours.

3 When ready to fry, combine the rice flour, white pepper, and ½ teaspoon of the salt in a shallow dish, for easy dredging.

4 Next, make the batter by whisking together the soy milk, mustard, remaining ½ teaspoon salt, black pepper, and togarashi in a shallow dish.

5 Line a plate with paper towels. Preheat a fryer to 375°F or heat ½ inch of the oil in a skillet or large

Canola oil for frying
Spicy Ketchup (below)

saucepan over high heat. One at a time, coat the pickles evenly, first in the dredge, then in the batter and then in the dredge once more before carefully placing in the oil to fry for about 2¹/₂ minutes or until golden brown on both sides.

6 Transfer to the paper towel–lined plate to absorb any excess oil. Arrange on a serving dish with spicy ketchup on the side for dipping.

SPICY KETCHUP

¹/₂ cup ketchup   2 tablespoons hot sauce

2 tablespoons barbecue sauce

Combine all of the ingredients in a small bowl and set aside. Refrigerate for up to 2 weeks.

MAKES ABOUT ¾ CUP

All great food cultures have their signature fritter: zeppole, falafel, hush puppies; frying is universal. In India, the fritter of choice is the pakora, a mixture of various ingredients bound with a little chickpea flour and fried up for a tasty snack. Nowadays, you'll see pakora throughout South Asia with countless riffs and variations. By using grated potato and some fresh herbs and spices, this particular version is at once rich and decadent but also fresh and aromatic. And the sweet-and-sour flavor of the tamarind sauce is a great accent, making your taste buds go haywire with a bright burst of tang against the crispy, little goodness.
SERVES 6 TO 8

POTATO PAKORA WITH TAMARIND SAUCE

2 cups chickpea flour

1 teaspoon cumin

1 teaspoon coriander

1 tablespoon curry powder

1/4 teaspoon turmeric

1 1/2 teaspoons sea salt

1/4 cup sunflower oil

2 cups peeled, grated potato (squeezed to remove excess water)

1/4 cup thinly sliced onion

1/4 cup chopped scallions (white parts only)

2 tablespoons chopped cilantro

1/2 cup tamarind paste (see tip)

2 tablespoons olive oil

1/4 cup sambal oelek

2 tablespoons agave syrup

2 tablespoons sugar

2 tablespoons lime juice

Canola oil for frying

1 Sift together the chickpea flour, cumin, coriander, curry powder, turmeric, and 1 teaspoon of the salt in a large bowl. Stir in 1 3/4 cups warm water and the sunflower oil, then add the potato, onion, scallions, and cilantro.

2 Whisk together the remaining ingredients except the canola oil in a medium bowl until smooth. Set aside.

3 Line a plate with paper towels. Preheat a fryer to 375°F or heat 1/2 inch of canola oil in a large skillet or saucepan. Using clean, lightly floured hands, roll the mixture into 1 1/2-inch balls. You should get about 18 out of the batch. Carefully fry the pakora, 3 or 4 at a time, for 3 minutes or until golden brown on all sides, turning occasionally. Transfer to the paper towel–lined plate to absorb any excess oil, then serve immediately with the tamarind sauce drizzled on top or on the side for dipping.

THREE OTHER USES FOR TAMARIND PASTE

1. Puree 1 cup in a blender with ¼ cup sugar and ½ cup water to use as a syrup for rum punch.

2. Combine ½ cup with ⅓ cup sunflower oil, 2 tablespoons agave, and 1 tablespoon tamari for an excellent sweet/sour grilling glaze.

3. Swap it for the orange juice in the Orange Granita (page 145) and churn it into a sorbet.

Happy hour is a fun, experimental playground for us. It's also the time we introduce new ethnic snacks that may end up on our regular menus. Scallion pancakes were an early addition, one that continues to surface as a crowd favorite, and we've developed a quick version that includes a bit of yeasted dough to achieve a great texture without all the tedious folding of a traditional laminated dough recipe. They cook up fat and fluffy, and they're quite easy to make at home. Serve them as snacks, or prepare an extra-large pancake and stuff it with seared mushrooms for a badass breakfast sandwich (see tip, opposite). For the ponzu, have some fun; experiment with different chiles, change up the citrus and use grapefruit or yuzu, or try a fine chiffonade of Kaffir lime leaves or lemongrass! **SERVES 4 TO 6**

SCALLION PANCAKES WITH CITRUS PONZU

1 teaspoon active dry yeast

1 teaspoon sugar

1½ cups all-purpose flour plus more for dusting

2 teaspoons sea salt

1 teaspoon white pepper

2 tablespoons sunflower oil, plus more for greasing and searing

½ cup plus 1 tablespoon finely chopped scallions (green parts only)

¼ cup tamari

2 tablespoons rice wine vinegar

1 tablespoon sesame oil

¼ teaspoon lemon zest

1 tablespoon lemon juice

2 teaspoons minced ginger

2 teaspoons agave syrup

1 Combine the yeast with ½ cup warm water and the sugar in a small bowl, then set aside for 10 minutes to activate.

2 Sift ¾ cup of the flour into the yeast mixture and stir until a loose dough forms.

3 Bring ½ cup water to a boil. Sift together the remaining ¾ cup flour with the salt and white pepper in a large bowl. Carefully stir in the boiling water to create a thick dough, then mix in 2 tablespoons of the sunflower oil. Transfer to a lightly floured work surface and knead together into a loose dough. Form into a ball, transfer to a lightly greased bowl, cover with a clean dish towel, and set aside to proof for 30 minutes.

4 Transfer the dough to a lightly floured work surface, knead ½ cup of the scallions into the dough ball. Cut the dough into 2-inch round balls and roll them each into small pancakes about 1½ inches thick.

5 Make the ponzu by whisking together the tamari, rice wine vinegar, sesame oil, lemon zest, lemon juice, ginger, remaining scallions, and agave. Set aside.

6 Line a plate with paper towels. Heat a shallow layer of sunflower oil in a large sauté pan or skillet over medium heat. Sear the pancakes, 4 to 6 at a time without overcrowding the pan, until golden brown on each side, about 3 minutes. Transfer to the paper towel–lined plate to absorb any excess oil, and serve immediately with the ponzu for dipping.

———

To turn this recipe into a breakfast sandwich, make one big pancake and stack it with seared shiitake mushrooms, finish with some Hoisin Sauce (page 23), and douse with a yuzu hollandaise of vegan mayo, mustard, salt, pepper, yuzu juice, and chives.

Chips and dip: classic, and every culture has its take. There's hummus and pita, tortilla chips and guac, British chips and tartar sauce . . . From time to time, we'll run an Indian take on chips and dip using crunchy papadums (thin and crispy lentil crackers) with a cold, creamy version of dal (stewed beans and lentils). The trick is to keep the dal super light so it doesn't snap the papadums. **SERVES 6 TO 8**

PAPADUMS WITH WHIPPED DAL

Canola oil for frying

12 papadums

1 tablespoon sunflower oil

1/4 cup chopped white onion

1 teaspoon minced garlic

1 teaspoon curry powder

1/8 teaspoon cardamom

1 teaspoon chopped ginger

1/2 teaspoon sea salt

1/2 teaspoon freshly ground
    black pepper

1 cup red lentils

1/4 cup cilantro leaves

1 1/2 tablespoons lemon juice

2 tablespoons chopped tomato

1/2 cup vegan mayo

1 Line a plate with paper towels. Pour a shallow layer of canola oil in a large sauté pan or skillet and heat over high heat until it ripples.

2 Fry the papadum sheets one at a time until crispy, about 30 seconds. There's no need to flip them, as they are so thin. Transfer to the paper towel–lined plate to absorb excess oil, then cool to room temperature. Store in an airtight container at room temperature for up to 2 days.

3 Heat the sunflower oil in a medium saucepan over high heat until it ripples. Add the onion, garlic, curry, cardamom, ginger, salt, and pepper and cook, stirring occasionally, until the onion is translucent, about 4 minutes.

4 Reduce the heat to medium, add 3 cups water and the lentils, and cook, stirring occasionally, until the lentils are tender, about 15 minutes. Set aside to cool fully.

5 Transfer the lentil mixture to a blender with the remaining ingredients and blend until smooth. Serve with papadum pieces or store in an airtight container in the refrigerator for up to 3 days.

Hong Kong is a fascinating mix of modern Western influence contrasted with ancient Chinese roots. Amid all the high-rises and hawkers, the junk ships and neon, food is everywhere. But we were looking up as we were in search of Hutong, a restaurant whose website pictures had captivated us for years and which had now become almost mythical in our minds. After crossing the harbor on the famous Star Ferry to Kowloon we finally found it and it did not disappoint. Especially the view.

Here we feasted on classic and nouveau Chinese dishes, all while taking in one of the greatest views on Earth. A highlight was a vegetarian version of turnip cake, which is usually made with sausage. The rich, glutinous, and creamy texture was a revelation, and we were instantly addicted. Our version is a little softer than the original; we prefer the extra-creamy, almost custard-like interior, and we fold in a little daikon radish to add a touch of funk.
SERVES 6 TO 8

TURNIP CAKES WITH HONSHIMEJI XO

2 cups shredded turnips

1 cup shredded daikon

1 cup shredded russet potato

½ cup diced shiitake mushroom caps

¼ teaspoon five-spice powder

¾ teaspoon sea salt

3 teaspoons sesame oil

½ cup Shiitake Dashi (page 130)

2 tablespoons potato starch (substitute cornstarch)

¼ cup rice flour

¼ cup sliced scallions (white and green parts)

½ cup chopped honshimeji mushrooms (substitute chopped button mushrooms)

½ cup XO Sauce (page 200)

1 Bring a large pot of salted water to a boil over high heat. Blanch the shredded turnips, daikon, and potato just until tender, about 4 minutes. Drain the vegetables, but do not rinse.

2 Add the shiitake mushroom caps, five-spice powder, and ¼ teaspoon of the salt to a medium bowl and toss to combine. Heat 1½ teaspoons of the sesame oil in a large sauté pan over high heat and sear the mushrooms until brown and crispy, about 5 minutes.

3 Meanwhile, whisk together the dashi with the potato starch, rice flour, and remaining ½ teaspoon salt in a small bowl.

4 Preheat the oven to 400°F. Line a sheet pan with parchment paper. Combine the shredded vegetables in a large bowl with the seared shiitakes, dashi mixture, and scallions until well combined. Spread onto the prepared sheet pan, cover with foil, and bake for 15 minutes. Remove the foil and bake, uncovered, until the cake is firm and golden brown on top, about 5 additional minutes.

5 Heat the remaining 1½ teaspoons sesame oil in a medium saucepan over high heat. Sear the honshimeji mushrooms until crispy, about 5 minutes. Allow to cool, then fold into the XO sauce.

6 Remove the turnip cake from the oven, slice into squares, and serve immediately, topped with honshimeji XO sauce. Store any leftover sauce, refrigerated, in an airtight container, for up to 5 days.

Latin America's answer to poutine, this is a kitchen-sink French fry dish traditionally topped with everything you need to die young, from meat to mayo. The selection of toppings can vary from country to country, region to region, and even food stand to food stand. Our version, while still hearty and not an everyday dish, is created with toppings from around the cookbook as well as a green chile crema and some marinated black beans. **SERVES 4 TO 6**

SALCHIPAPAS

5 to 6 Kennebec or Yukon Gold
    potatoes

Canola oil for frying

Salt

Carrot Asado (page 70)

Achiote-Marinated Black Beans
    (opposite)

Curtido (page 96)

Sliced avocado

Green Chile Crema (opposite)

Cilantro

1 Scrub the potatoes and cut into ¼- to ½-inch slices using a mandolin.

2 Fill a deep pan with 2 inches of the oil and heat to 375°F until the oil begins to ripple. Carefully add the potato slices a few at a time, removing them just as they turn gold, 2 to 3 minutes. Allow to cool, or refrigerate until ready to use.

3 When ready to serve, fry the potatoes again (same temperature) until golden brown and crispy. Remove from the oil onto a plate lined with paper towels. Season them lightly with salt.

4 Arrange the potatoes in 4 to 6 separate bowls or in one large bowl as a centerpiece.

5 Cut the carrots crosswise into 1-inch-thick coins.

6 Arrange the beans, curtido, carrots, and avocado in four sections on top of the fries.

7 Drizzle with the green chile crema and garnish with cilantro leaves.

ACHIOTE-MARINATED BLACK BEANS

One 15.5-ounce can black beans, drained and rinsed

¼ cup minced red onion

½ cup minced tomato

¼ cup chopped cilantro

1 tablespoon chopped mint

¼ cup fresh lime juice

1 tablespoon sunflower or peanut oil

½ teaspoon sea salt

1 teaspoon achiote paste or ground annatto seed

1 teaspoon cumin

Combine all of the ingredients in a bowl and let marinate for at least 1 hour or refrigerate for up to 2 days.

MAKES 3 CUPS

GREEN CHILE CREMA

½ cup packed chopped cilantro

2 jalapeños, deseeded

2 poblano peppers, deseeded

2 long hot peppers, deseeded

¼ cup sunflower oil

1 cup vegan sour cream

1 teaspoon freshly ground black pepper

2 teaspoons sea salt

1 teaspoon cumin

Combine all of the ingredients in a food processor and pulse until creamy.

MAKES 2 CUPS

We like to lean toward simplicity and clean flavors. So every time we start a jerk dish with a blank canvas, it's always a riot how long the list of ingredients grows. The point is that jerk is a very complex blend of spices that must work in a perfect harmony of herbal, sweet, spicy, and sour. It takes many parts to complete the whole and nothing can be out of sync. These cashews have made many appearances on our menus over the years but most recently played a great supporting role alongside our Jerk Trumpet Mushrooms (page 20). They are terrific on top of a salad or just for snacking. **SERVES 4 TO 6 AS A PARTY SNACK OR 8 TO 10 AS A SALAD ADDITION**

JERK-SPICED CASHEWS

2 cups unsalted cashews

1 tablespoon sunflower oil

1 tablespoon Jerk Spice (below)

1 Preheat the oven to 350°F. Toss the cashews lightly with the sunflower oil in a medium bowl. Sprinkle with jerk spice to taste.

2 Spread the cashews in a single layer on a baking tray.

3 Bake for about 4 minutes, until the cashews are lightly golden brown. Allow to cool completely before serving. Store in an airtight container for up to 1 week.

JERK SPICE

1 tablespoon sea salt

2 tablespoons freshly ground black pepper

1½ tablespoons allspice

¼ teaspoon plus ⅛ teaspoon ground cloves

¾ teaspoon nutmeg

1½ teaspoons cayenne pepper

1½ teaspoons cumin

1½ teaspoons curry powder

¾ teaspoon cinnamon

Combine all of the ingredients in a small bowl until thoroughly mixed. Store in an airtight container for up to 2 weeks.

This very simple and addictive recipe will most likely become part of your weekly snack repertoire. Think honey-roasted peanuts, only we're using agave syrup and jazzing things up with a touch of sriracha. You could eat these solo, fold them into some badass granola, or you could incorporate them into dessert the way we do with our Chocolate–Peanut Butter Waffles (page 166). **MAKES ½ CUP**

SRIRACHA PEANUTS

2 tablespoons agave syrup

2 tablespoons sriracha

¼ teaspoon sea salt

¼ teaspoon white pepper

1 cup roasted peanuts, chopped

1 Whisk together the agave, sriracha, salt, and white pepper in a small mixing bowl.

2 Heat a large sauté pan over medium heat. Toast the peanuts until they are warmed evenly and starting to brown, about 3 minutes. Remove from the heat and stir in the sriracha mixture until the peanuts are evenly coated. When fully cool, transfer to an airtight container and store at room temperature for up to 1 week.

QUEBEC CITY FESTIVAL STAND

We grew up going to carnivals and fairs that were full of cotton candy and hot dogs, funnel cake and French fries. Back then, it seemed magical— all the sights and smells and sugar highs. We had a bit of a flashback when we were stomping through a fairground on Ile d'Orleans in the Saint Lawrence River just outside Quebec City. Here were people selling artisanal jams and fancy mustards and tasting tables offering local wines, and the food memory we cherish the most was the boiled corn.

It was Labor Day weekend, a holiday celebrated in Canada at the same time as in the States, and corn is everywhere. In true laid-back and wholesome spirit, there was also a giant bar of communal butter supplied so carnival-goers could slather their corn with as much as they liked. But it didn't need anything—that corn was the most delicious, juicy, sweet pop of nutty flavor. We like to jazz things up at the restaurant by grilling and marinating, basting, and drizzling, but the corn on that day in that place was one of the simplest and best things we'd ever eaten. In the sweet end-of-summer air in rural French Canada, wholesome and unpretentious, eating outside with our hands—this was street food at its finest.

SALADS & SLAWS

Blackened Tofu Salad 52

Malaysian Cauliflower Salad 53

Moroccan Olive Salad 54

Hearts of Palm Slaw 55

Lomi Tomato Salad 55

Spicy Chaat Salad 56

Jerk Sweet Potato Salad 58

Hong Kong Chopped Salad 60

Chickpeas with Mint Chutney 62

Escoveitch Cabbage 63

Mexican Cobb 65

Bean Bhajji 66

共
和黨總統候選人辯論的重點少不了
⋯⋯經濟與四年前相比已改善不少⋯⋯
國人並不⋯⋯根據華爾街日報
⋯BC最近民調，有半數受訪者不
⋯可總統處理經濟的方式

眾對前景不敢奢望

008年美國經濟大衰退時，很
⋯住房⋯⋯
⋯⋯離經

經濟問題纏繞難解

⋯⋯「解人們真實的經濟情
⋯⋯有以下三個因素。

1) 收入不比1995年時多

⋯⋯經通貨膨脹調整後，美國家庭
⋯⋯和1995年時一樣，這意味著
⋯⋯一般家庭沒有比20年
⋯⋯這就是為什麼這次選舉

圖：美國目前經濟難題包括調漲最低工資，
兼職工過多與民眾消費意願低等。圖為⋯
關瑪商選。

今天的孩子長大後財務狀況比父母
糟的選民⋯

中產低工資與前景不平等引發這麼
多的潮論。

2) 太多的兼職工

自從奧巴馬總統上台後，失業
率確實下降了很多，但是美國有「隱
性失業」的問題，即超過660萬人從
事兼職工作，卻渴望有全職工作，
這比經濟大衰退前的480萬兼職工，
高出許多。

調強「最低工資」的最大好處就
是這些兼職工可以有全職工作，伴
隨著享有福利與收入保障，據統計，

美小型油商或爆倒閉潮

(Getty Images)

務公司思維特(Swift Worldwide
Resources)估計，全球⋯
年以來巴裁員17.61萬人，高於6
月中估計的15萬人，其中6月和7
⋯計劃年底前每月裁員人數持平⋯
⋯毛油價跌破50美元/桶⋯
⋯油投資者及服務公司還⋯也許
⋯田服務業⋯今年以交易受青
⋯如果油價持續升彈炸開
⋯款申請書，這個速度讓
⋯行業，該機構石油和
⋯的流動性指數6月
⋯加3.8%，未來一年經⋯
⋯升。◇

3) 人們不願消費

美國人向來⋯
名，因⋯農⋯他們會繼續儲蓄
⋯要那麼不願花錢，這是一個真正
的問題，因為美國經濟中消費支出
佔約70%。這反映了人們對未來⋯
⋯高達5%以上，比經濟衰退時3%至
⋯增加。

⋯經濟專家⋯最近消費支出增⋯
⋯尤其是汽車消費及出⋯
⋯但事實⋯之後的⋯

目前美國經濟是⋯
可以放寬⋯日本，但美國代表⋯
的⋯本⋯規模⋯2015⋯有望⋯
落⋯2%至2.8%之間⋯

特別是(Donald Trump)民調⋯
的部分原因是他的競選口號「讓⋯
國再次強大」(Make America Great
Again)，彷彿是奧巴馬當年的競選
口號「希望」(Hope)，它有對抗好⋯
來的多層次內涵，尤其是經濟方面⋯
奧巴馬執政期間是有不少經濟⋯
問題，那麼共和黨的答案是甚麼？◇

裁員工生活貧困的可能性也同行
業工的五倍。

繪圖芯片熱銷
Nvidia盤後飆漲

⋯⋯(Nvidia)第一季⋯
11.5億美元，大幅⋯
⋯遜8%，第二季⋯
⋯分析師預期⋯超過出⋯
⋯額9.2%，至22.43美元⋯

⋯據路透社報導⋯
⋯是看用的⋯
⋯片，市場⋯
⋯不可⋯股股⋯
⋯如⋯專用(AMD)⋯

⋯但⋯在主力⋯
GeForce⋯
⋯收⋯報⋯
Securities的分析師⋯(Betty
Hou)估計，PC遊戲芯片⋯
⋯銷⋯

⋯此外，美偉⋯力芯⋯
⋯中國剛研小數上的芯⋯
⋯電汽車的⋯器⋯且是⋯
⋯部⋯季⋯稅⋯80%，增⋯
⋯較占比達6.2%。

⋯邊⋯日前⋯巴⋯
⋯汽車⋯其芯⋯
⋯機⋯人⋯
⋯芯片⋯最新⋯進⋯
⋯效占⋯
⋯如此⋯美偉⋯

30年固

【大紀元記者⋯報導】由於美
⋯加息的不確定是使美國債殖利⋯
⋯低，抵押貸款利率再次下降⋯
⋯兩週跌至4%以下，據房地美
(Freddie Mac)每周對125家放⋯
⋯的調查顯示，平均30年期固⋯
⋯巴利率為3.91%，上週為3.98%，
而一年前降4.14%。

房貸利率於2011年首次低於
4%，2012年底時跌到3.31%的
低位。這項周調查自1971年以來⋯
目前30年期利率降到6月4日以
低位。

91%

When you think of Riviera Maya, you might think of Cancun and shots of tequila, but more and more, people are venturing south to explore the ancient ruins and get a more peaceful snapshot of life along Mexico's Yucatan Peninsula. Tulum is the new not-so-secret hot spot, known for its glorious white sand beach, yoga retreats, and simple bungalows with nothing built higher than a palm tree. We fell instantly in love with this charming little surf town and count the beach among our favorites in the world. Life seems simple here, and so does the food. This salad is the perfect après-sun meal—all you need is an ice-cold bottle of Negra Modelo! **SERVES 4**

BLACKENED TOFU SALAD

2 tablespoons tamari

½ cup sunflower oil

3 tablespoons blackening seasoning

One 16-ounce block firm tofu, sliced into 4 slabs

⅛ cup lime juice

2 teaspoons sherry vinegar

2 teaspoons Dijon mustard

⅓ cup olive oil

1 teaspoon sea salt

1 teaspoon freshly ground black pepper

½ teaspoon cumin

½ cup roughly chopped cilantro

¼ cup chopped onion

1 garlic clove

4 cups chopped romaine lettuce

½ cup diced avocado

½ cup diced tomato

½ cup diced red onion

½ cup grilled corn kernels

¼ cup diced poblano pepper

1 Whisk together the tamari, sunflower oil, and blackening seasoning in a small bowl. Arrange the slabs of tofu on a sheet pan or in a shallow dish and pour the marinade over the tofu, coating all sides evenly. Refrigerate for 2 hours.

2 Combine the lime juice, vinegar, mustard, olive oil, salt, pepper, cumin, cilantro, onion, and garlic in a food processor. Pulse until all of the cilantro is broken down and the mixture is the consistency of a loose vinaigrette. This can be stored in the refrigerator for up to 3 days.

3 Toss the romaine with the vinaigrette in a medium bowl, then arrange on serving dishes with the avocado, tomato, red onion, corn, and poblano in different sections.

4 Remove the tofu from the refrigerator. Preheat a chargrill to high (a grill pan will work too). Grill the tofu, brushing once with leftover marinade, until you achieve a nice hashtag pattern on both sides, 3 to 4 minutes per side. Place the tofu on top of the salads and serve.

It's impossible to categorize Malaysian cooking in any neat and concise way—it's a conglomeration of different food cultures converging across the peninsula. Between the more tropical notes of traditional Malay cooking and the aromatics of Indian influence, plus the techniques and ingredients of nearby Thailand, there's a lot going on. To call this dish a salad is almost unfair, as its heat and intensity immediately get in your face and don't let go. **SERVES 4**

MALAYSIAN CAULIFLOWER SALAD

4 cups cauliflower florets

½ teaspoon sea salt

2 tablespoons sesame oil

1 tablespoon tamari

1 tablespoon sambal oelek
(see tip, below)

½ teaspoon chile oil, optional

¼ teaspoon white pepper

1 teaspoon lime juice

1 teaspoon sugar

4 cups shredded iceberg lettuce

¼ cup chopped scallions
(white parts only)

¼ cup chopped peanuts

¼ cup chopped cilantro

¼ cup chopped basil

1 Preheat the oven to 400°F. Toss the cauliflower with the salt and the sesame oil. Arrange on a sheet pan and roast until golden brown, about 10 minutes. Remove from the oven and set aside to cool fully.

2 Combine the tamari, sambal oelek, chile oil (if using), white pepper, lime juice, and sugar in a large bowl, whisking together until smooth. Toss the cauliflower in the dressing until evenly coated, then let sit for at least 15 minutes.

3 Arrange the iceberg lettuce on a serving dish, then pile the dressed cauliflower on top. Sprinkle with scallions, peanuts, cilantro, and basil, and serve.

THREE OTHER USES FOR SAMBAL OELEK

1. Sprinkle a small spoonful atop any Asian soup.

2. Mix 2 teaspoons with 1 tablespoon tamari, 2 tablespoons sesame oil, and 2 teaspoons rice wine vinegar to make a spicy Asian vinaigrette for any vegetables, whether fresh or cooked.

3. Anytime you're cooking with coconut milk, sambal is the perfect spice to balance the richness.

The small winding streets of Marrakech's medina are like an Indiana Jones movie set. At least that's how it felt to us when we touched down on a rainy night in March. Our first food experience was tucked inside the peaceful walls of our riad (a hotel converted from an elegant sanctuary-style home built around a lush courtyard): enjoying a multicourse Moroccan feast of harira, Moroccan salads, and tagine, plus a little local wine.

The scene was magical, but the star of the meal was quite simple: olives. They came out with the salads, in a little dish, swimming ever so slightly in a little argan oil tinted with harissa. These were the most delicious olives we had ever sampled, fresh and ripe in texture and bursting with a flavor that didn't overpower their natural fruitiness. We knew then and there that our Moroccan food adventure would be a good one. **SERVES 8**

MOROCCAN OLIVE SALAD

4 cups pitted picholine olives, halved (substitute any green olive)

1 teaspoon Harissa (page 74)

½ teaspoon ground cumin

⅛ teaspoon cinnamon

½ teaspoon paprika

½ teaspoon orange zest

2 teaspoons olive oil

1 teaspoon food-grade argan oil or sunflower oil

1 teaspoon lemon juice

1 tablespoon chopped cilantro

1 Combine all of the ingredients in a large bowl and toss until the olives are well coated.

2 Transfer to an airtight container and store in the refrigerator for up to 1 week.

These two salads feature produce and techniques from beautiful Hawaii. We have our hearts of palm flown in from the big island, and lomi means massage, which is what we do to the tomatoes. Both of these dishes are delicious on their own or atop our Huli Huli Barbecue Seitan Tacos (page 99).

HEARTS OF PALM SLAW

1 cup shredded hearts of palm

1 cup shredded green cabbage

2 tablespoons thinly sliced red onion

1 tablespoon chopped scallions (green and white parts)

1 teaspoon lemon juice

1 teaspoon sherry vinegar

1 teaspoon Dijon mustard

2 tablespoons vegan mayo

1 teaspoon olive oil

¼ teaspoon cumin

½ teaspoon sea salt

½ teaspoon freshly ground black pepper

Combine all of the ingredients in a medium bowl until the vegetables are evenly coated. Transfer to an airtight container and store in the refrigerator for up to 3 days.

MAKES 1½ CUPS

LOMI TOMATO SALAD

¾ cup diced tomato

⅓ cup diced red onion

¼ cup chopped scallions (white parts only)

½ teaspoon sea salt

¼ teaspoon freshly ground black pepper

1 teaspoon olive oil

Combine all of the ingredients in a medium bowl until the vegetables are evenly coated. Be gentle; this is a subtle way of working seasoning into every nook and cranny and helping the vegetables release their own juices into the dressing. Leftovers can be stored in the refrigerator for up to 3 days.

MAKES 1 CUP

When you think of street food, your mind may focus on lots of crispy, fried snacks—you might not think of salads. But a chaat salad is a nice exception. North Indian in origin, chaat is a term used all over Asia to describe fried or crunchy snack foods like kara boondi (tiny lentil puffs) or rice crisps. These are the crunchy element to any good chaat salad. Our version focuses on three classic ingredients: crunchy papadums, chickpeas, and potatoes, resulting in a bright, colorful, and hearty salad that can be enjoyed on its own or as a side dish of a larger meal. **SERVES 4**

SPICY CHAAT SALAD

⅓ cup vegan mayo

1 tablespoon Dijon mustard

1 teaspoon rice wine vinegar

½ teaspoon curry powder

¼ teaspoon cumin

⅛ teaspoon cardamon

⅛ teaspoon coriander

¼ teaspoon mustard powder (see tip, below)

¼ teaspoon chili powder

¼ teaspoon tamarind paste

¼ teaspoon minced ginger

4 cups chopped romaine lettuce

¼ cup slivered red onion

¼ cup julienned cucumber

¼ cup julienned carrot

¼ cup diced tomato

1 cup canned chickpeas, drained and rinsed

½ cup diced baked potato, ¼-inch dice

1 tablespoon chopped cilantro

½ cup crushed papadums

1 Whisk together the vegan mayo, Dijon mustard, vinegar, curry powder, cumin, cardamom, coriander, mustard powder, chili powder, tamarind paste, and ginger in a small bowl.

2 In a large bowl combine the romaine with the red onion, cucumber, carrot, tomato, chickpeas, potato, and cilantro. Add the dressing, a small amount at a time, and mix again, ensuring everything is just evenly coated.

3 Transfer to serving dishes and sprinkle with papadums to serve.

THREE OTHER USES FOR MUSTARD POWDER

1. Stir a little into curries for a punchy, sour note.

2. Whisk 1 tablespoon per cup into simple vinaigrettes to add body.

3. Add 1 tablespoon per cup to potato salad along with vegan mayonnaise to make it extra creamy and mustardy!

At V Street, we love potatoes, whether they're russets or fingerlings, Yukon Golds or Peruvian Purples—or, in this case, sweet potatoes spiked with a little jerk seasoning. This cold potato salad is perfect in the summertime with Jerk Trumpet Mushrooms (page 20), a little Escoveitch Cabbage (page 63), and some Jerk-Spiced Cashews (page 46) for an amazing Jamaican picnic. **SERVES 4 TO 6**

JERK SWEET POTATO SALAD

3 cups ½-inch-diced sweet potato

2 bay leaves

¼ cup diced celery

¼ cup diced red onion

½ cup vegan mayo

2 tablespoons Dijon mustard

1 teaspoon Jerk Spice (page 46)

1 teaspoon sea salt

1 teaspoon freshly ground black pepper

1 Bring a large pot of salted water to a boil over high heat. Add the sweet potatoes with the bay leaves and cook just until tender, about 8 minutes.

2 Drain the sweet potatoes, discarding the bay leaves, then spread the potatoes on a sheet pan to cool for 15 minutes.

3 Combine the remaining ingredients in a medium bowl. Fold the cooled potatoes into the dressing and serve. Leftovers can be stored in an airtight container in the refrigerator for up to 3 days.

When we arrived in Hong Kong, we went right to "work." Our first meal was in a "tofu restaurant," a shabby little storefront near our hotel. We ordered wok-fried tofu, seared bok choy with garlic sauce, and an oozy bowl of stir-fried eggplant. And so the trip went on like this, but after bingeing on all sorts of heavy Chinese dishes, we did find ourselves wishing for something fresh, cleansing, and light . . . like a salad! So here we've assembled a lunch entrée salad with Asian-leaning ingredients that stand up perfectly against the creamy Szechuan peppercorn ranch dressing, a Chinese twist on an American classic. **SERVES 4**

HONG KONG CHOPPED SALAD

1 cup vegan mayo

⅓ cup Dijon mustard

1 teaspoon crushed Szechuan peppercorns

1 teaspoon minced shallots

½ teaspoon minced garlic

½ teaspoon tamari

1 teaspoon rice wine vinegar

3 cups chopped Romaine lettuce

3 cups mixed greens

½ cup thinly sliced red cabbage

½ cup shelled, blanched edamame beans

½ cup Chòu Dòufu (page 26)

¼ cup shredded red radish

¼ cup chopped watermelon radish (substitute daikon)

¼ cup chopped scallions (green parts only)

1 tablespoon black sesame seeds

1 Whisk together the vegan mayo, mustard, peppercorns, shallots, garlic, tamari, and vinegar in a small bowl until smooth. (Leftovers can be stored in the refrigerator for up to 5 days.)

2 Combine the remaining vegetables and the Chòu Dòufu in a large bowl and gently toss with the salad dressing until evenly coated.

3 Sprinkle with the black sesame seeds and serve.

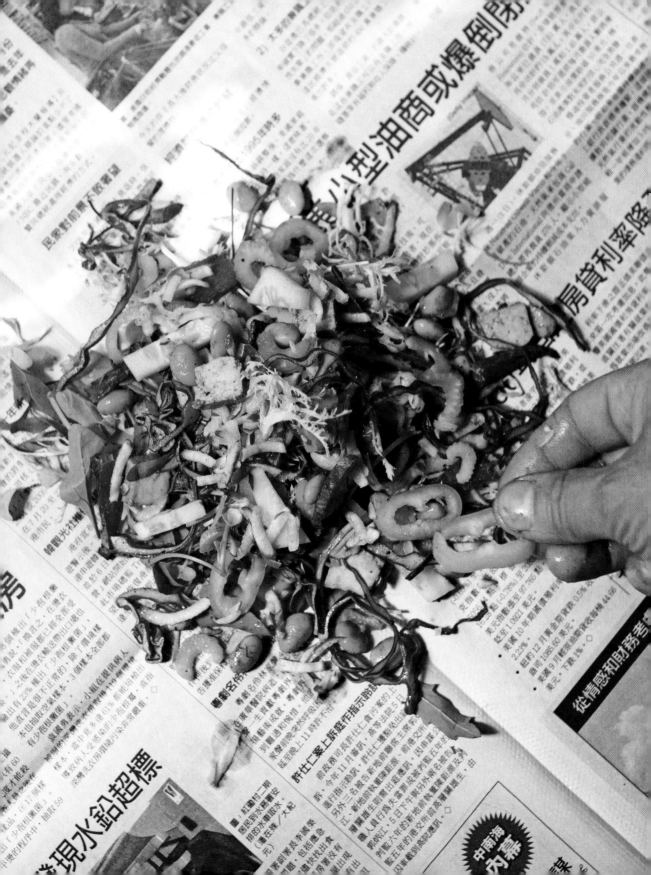

What Indian chefs do with spices is quite remarkable. For us, there is nothing like a good curry experience where the chefs just nail the flavors with the right amount of heat and spice. We created this simple salad to highlight the lighter side of Indian cuisine, something you could have perhaps on a summer day or as a side dish for dinner. The chutney here is light and bright and full of fiery green chile. **MAKES 4 CUPS**

CHICKPEAS WITH MINT CHUTNEY

2 cups of canned chickpeas, drained and rinsed

½ cup finely diced red onion

¼ cup diced tomatoes

MINT CHUTNEY

6 long hot peppers, stems and seeds removed, grilled

2 poblano peppers, stems and seeds removed, grilled

1 cup chopped onion

2 garlic cloves

1 tablespoon minced ginger

1 bunch cilantro

2 tablespoons lemon juice

¼ cup sunflower oil

2 teaspoons sea salt

1 teaspoon freshly ground black pepper

¼ cup mint leaves, packed

1 teaspoon cumin

½ teaspoon cardamom

1 teaspoon sugar

1 Combine the chickpeas, red onion, and tomatoes in a medium bowl.

2 Add all of the ingredients for the mint chutney to a food processor with ¼ cup water. Pulse until it reaches a pesto-like consistency.

3 Serve the chickpeas with the chutney alongside or tossed together. Leftovers will keep in the refrigerator for 3 days.

You might already be familiar with Latin escabeche, a cooking method popular in Spain and Portugal. It's essentially a quick hot-pickling process, and it's been adapted around the world over the years. In Jamaica, the locals call it escoveitch, and it typically includes some spicy Scotch bonnet peppers, onions, and other spices along with some sharp vinegar. Here we took that idea and prepared a slaw-style condiment, one that can be used on tacos, in salads, or on bowls of beans and rice. And since the Scotch bonnet peppers are, of course, the hallmark of a good escoveitch, watch out—it's spicy! **MAKES 2 CUPS**

ESCOVEITCH CABBAGE

2 tablespoons sunflower oil

¼ teaspoon minced garlic

1 cup shredded green cabbage

¼ cup peeled carrot, julienned

¼ cup thinly sliced onion

¼ cup thinly sliced Scotch bonnet (substitute jalapeño or poblano)

1 tablespoon white vinegar

¼ teaspoon sugar

¼ teaspoon red chile flakes

¼ teaspoon sea salt

¼ teaspoon freshly ground black pepper

¼ teaspoon allspice

⅛ teaspoon cumin

1 Heat the sunflower oil in a large sauté pan over high heat. Add the garlic. Just as the garlic toasts and turns brown, 1 to 2 minutes, add the cabbage, carrot, onion, and Scotch bonnet pepper. Sear, stirring occasionally, just until the vegetables become tender, about 2 minutes.

2 Deglaze the pan by adding the vinegar and stirring up any solids that have stuck to the pan. Reduce completely until the vinegar has evaporated, then transfer to a large bowl.

3 Add the remaining ingredients to the bowl and stir to combine, until the salad is evenly coated. Allow to cool fully before transferring to an airtight container. Store in the refrigerator for up to 5 days.

The classic American Cobb salad and Mexican tortilla salad are probably two of Americans' favorite ways to eat their greens. We pay homage to both in this fun fusion entrée salad. The real inspiration for this dish came from tlayuda, one of the best things we have ever eaten in Mexico, right on the beach. It was a very thin, crispy corn dough topped with an amazingly fresh array of local produce including avocado, corn, zucchini, and green chiles. Tlayuda is one of those dishes that you have never heard of before but once you try it, you wonder how you have ever lived life without it. Feel free to improvise and add whatever vegetables you like or have in your fridge; the tangy cilantro dressing will hold up to anything you can throw at it!
SERVES 4

MEXICAN COBB

½ cup cilantro leaves

½ cup lime juice

2 teaspoons sherry vinegar

2 teaspoons Dijon mustard

⅔ cup olive oil

1 teaspoon sea salt

½ teaspoon cumin

¼ cup chopped shallots

1 teaspoon minced garlic

1 cup black bean puree
   (page 94)

Four 6-inch corn tortillas
   (freshly fried or baked)

6 cups chopped romaine lettuce

1 avocado, diced

1 cup Curtido (page 96)

1 cup sliced Carrot Asado
   (page 70)

1 cup diced fresh tomatoes

¼ cup finely chopped red onion

1 Place the cilantro, lime juice, vinegar, mustard, olive oil, salt, cumin, shallots, and garlic in a food processor and pulse just until the cilantro leaves are torn, about 20 seconds. Any leftovers can be stored in the refrigerator for up to 3 days.

2 When ready to serve, spread the black bean puree on top of the corn tortillas and arrange on serving dishes.

3 Dress the lettuce with the vinaigrette as desired in a medium bowl, then arrange the greens on top of the tortillas.

4 Arrange the other ingredients in small piles on top of the greens and serve with any remaining vinaigrette on the side.

Traditionally, bhajjis are a type of fritter you'd find throughout parts of Southern India. Similiar to pakoras, they can have any number of different ingredients and can range in texture from creamy and smooth to chock-full of vegetables. They're often fried, but not always. Bhajjis are typically bound with a little chickpea flour then fried, but we've put in a twist and left ours mashed and served cold like a rustic South Indian potato salad. This is great on its own, as a side dish, or stuffed in a wrap. **SERVES 4**

BEAN BHAJJI

3 cups green beans, trimmed and blanched

2 tablespoons tomato paste

½ teaspoon lime juice

2 tablespoons vegetable broth

2 tablespoons sunflower oil

¼ cup diced white onion

1 teaspoon minced garlic

2 teaspoons curry powder

½ teaspoon sea salt

¼ teaspoon turmeric

½ teaspoon smoked paprika

1 potato, baked and cut into 1-inch dice

¼ cup scallions (green parts only)

2 tablespoons chopped mint

¼ cup chopped cilantro

1 Blanch the green beans by dropping them in boiling water for about 3 minutes. Remove from the water, allow to cool, and cut into 1-inch pieces.

2 In a small mixing bowl, whisk together the tomato paste, lime juice, and vegetable broth.

3 Heat the oil in a large sauté pan over high heat, then add the onion, garlic, curry powder, salt, turmeric, and smoked paprika, reduce the heat to medium, and sauté until the onion is translucent, about 4 minutes. Add the green beans and sauté for 2 more minutes. Add the tomato paste mixture, stir until the beans are evenly coated, then remove from the heat.

4 Add the potatoes to the pan and mash lightly until they are chunky. Let cool fully in the refrigerator for at least 30 minutes. Then serve garnished with scallions, mint, and cilantro.

MARRAKECH NIGHT MARKET

Walking through the steamy passages of Marrakech's main night market, zigzagging between colorful tents under glittering tin lights, stepping through the wafts of some of the world's most fragrant street food, traversing Jemaa el-Fna is one of the most electrifying food experiences on the planet. Between the blaring sirens of the snake charmers and the eager hawkers selling their wares first in Arabic, then in French, switching over to English and German on occasion, it's a dizzying stroll as you approach the main marketplace. What is home to juice stands and shopkeepers peddling olives and scarves by day transforms at night into a wonderland of smoky skewers, crispy fritters, and fragrant tagines.

And how well can vegetarians eat in Marrakech? Pretty damn well, actually. In fact, it was one of the food experiences of a lifetime for us. It took a little convincing of the locals that we really were okay with only vegetables on our skewers, but between that, the Moroccan salads, the onion crepes, and the pastries, we ate like kings and queens. If you're looking for expert Moroccan cuisine, there are countless excellent restaurants in riads and hotels scattered through the medina, or, for a more rustic experience, head out to the mountains to sample some Berber cooking. But if you're looking for a jolt of exciting street food culture, you can't miss Jemaa el-Fna.

MARKET

Carrot Asado 70

Cauliflower 65 73

Harissa-Grilled Cauliflower 74

Mushroom Bulgogi 75

Kung Pao String Beans 76

Peruvian Fries 79

**Grilled Sweet Potatoes
with Black Vinegar** 81

Togarashi Home Fries 82

V Street Kimchi 85

**Za'atar-Grilled Corn
with Zhoug** 86

**Market Greens
with Pickled Turnips** 89

¡Vamos a un asado! *That's right—we're going to a barbecue! A Latin one, and we're gonna grill carrots! Yes, you can coax smoky, gamey flavors out of just about anything if you know what you're doing. And if you use the right ingredients, you can get a sticky, sweet, and tangy sauce that will impress the most devout carnivore. At V Street, we lacquer all kinds of veggies with the whole gamut of different sauces, spice blends, and marinades, and Carrot Asado is a fan favorite. By leaving the skins on (repeat, do not peel!) and roasting the carrots before grilling, you get a tender texture through the middle and an almost crispy skin on the outside. The effects are always outstanding, and the possibilities are truly endless. So grab some napkins and roll up your sleeves!* SERVES 4 TO 6

CARROT ASADO

8 to 10 medium carrots, trimmed

3 tablespoons sunflower oil

2 teaspoons Latin Spice Blend (page 210)

2 tablespoons rice wine vinegar

¼ teaspoon cumin

¼ teaspoon paprika

2 tablespoons tamari

2 teaspoons agave nectar

¼ cup ketchup

2 teaspoons molasses

1 Preheat the oven to 400°F. Place the carrots in a large bowl with 1 tablespoon of the sunflower oil and the Latin Spice Blend and toss to combine. Arrange the carrots in a single layer on a sheet pan and roast until just tender, about 15 minutes, depending on their size. Remove from the oven and set aside to cool fully.

2 Combine all of the remaining ingredients in a blender with ¼ cup water and blend until smooth. Transfer to an airtight container and store in the refrigerator for up to 1 week.

3 When ready to serve, heat a chargrill on high or a grill pan over high heat. Toss the carrots with the glaze, then grill until the sauce caramelizes and the carrots show char marks, turning once or twice, about 4 minutes. Serve immediately.

Our travels have not yet landed us in India, but that doesn't stop us from experimenting with the country's fascinating culinary traditions. From tandoor vegetables to stuffed breads, dried fruits to tangy stews, the repertoire of Indian cuisine is vast, to say the least. Our Cauliflower 65 is a riff off a traditional street food dish from Southern India called Chicken 65, fried chicken with lots of red chiles and other spices. We find the texture of the cauliflower a wonderfully willing agent for showcasing all the "65" flavors. This spicy dish is pretty perfect on its own, but it's also great over rice or stuffed in sandwiches. **SERVES 4**

CAULIFLOWER 65

½ cup ketchup

¼ cup sriracha

2 teaspoons minced ginger

¼ cup chopped cilantro

1 tablespoon plus 1 teaspoon
   rice wine vinegar

¼ cup vegan mayo

1 tablespoon plus 1 teaspoon
   curry powder

2 teaspoons cumin

1 teaspoon sea salt

2 teaspoons cayenne pepper

Canola oil for frying

1 cup cornstarch

3 cups cauliflower florets

1 Combine the ketchup, sriracha, ginger, cilantro, rice wine vinegar, mayo, curry powder, cumin, salt, and cayenne in a medium bowl. Whisk together until smooth (any leftovers can be kept in the refrigerator for up to 5 days).

2 Preheat a fryer to 375°F or heat ½ inch of the oil in a skillet or large saucepan over high heat. Add the cornstarch to a medium mixing bowl for dredging.

3 Line a plate with paper towels and set aside. Dunk the cauliflower florets in the sauce, then dredge in the cornstarch, making sure that each piece is evenly coated in liquid and dry ingredients. Transfer to a sheet pan and repeat with the remaining florets.

4 Fry the florets immediately in small batches until golden brown, about 2 minutes, depending on their size. Remove from the fryer and transfer to the paper towel–lined plate to absorb any excess oil, then serve.

Harissa is found all over Northern Africa and the Middle East. Each region has a different take on this spicy condiment, but we fell in love with the thick, lemony version we found in Marrakech. This is a great sauce to keep in your fridge—it can be customized to go with just about any cuisine. But it's at its peak when used for grilling—the smokiness from the chargrill is a perfect match for all the vinegar and spice. **SERVES 6 TO 8**

HARISSA-GRILLED CAULIFLOWER

HARISSA

1 cup chopped tomatoes

1 cup jarred Calabrian chile peppers, stems removed (substitute any pickled red chile)

4 garlic cloves, peeled

1 teaspoon coriander

1 teaspoon cumin

1 teaspoon caraway seed

1 tablespoon rice wine vinegar

1 teaspoon sea salt

2 tablespoons olive oil

2 heads cauliflower, stems and leaves removed

1 Combine all of the harissa ingredients in a food processor and pulse until just combined. Store any leftovers in an airtight container in the refrigerator for up to 2 weeks.

2 Bring a large pot of salted water to a rolling boil over high heat. Meanwhile, cut the cauliflower heads into 1-inch-thick steaks.

3 Blanch the cauliflower for 4 minutes, then remove from the water and drain.

4 Preheat a chargrill to high heat (a grill pan will work as well). Transfer the cauliflower to a sheet pan and brush with the harissa, evenly coating each cauliflower steak on all sides.

5 Grill the cauliflower until char marks appear, about 1 minute on each side. The cauliflower can be served immediately, or cooled to be reheated later.

Korean food is one of our comfort foods. We've come to love it through all the banchan (small little bowls of appetizers) and bowl after bowl of meat-free dolsot bibimbap (sizzling stone pot rice with marinated vegetables). That being said, bulgogi, or "Korean barbecue," is pretty off-limits to a vegetarian so we decided to make our own version with mushrooms. We find that mushrooms take extremely well to the technique of marinating and grilling, and the rest of the components are right from the classic barbecue feast. Trumpet mushrooms also work well for this process. If you are not a mushroom fan, try seitan, tofu, or eggplant.
SERVES 4

MUSHROOM BULGOGI

2 tablespoons gochujang

¼ cup sesame oil

1 tablespoon tamari

2 teaspoons minced ginger

2 teaspoons light brown sugar

¼ cup sliced scallions
   (white parts only)

4 large portobello caps,
   stems removed

8 butter lettuce leaves

¼ cup chopped cucumber

SIDES

¼ cup of each (pick and choose
   what you like): sliced pickled
   or raw hot peppers, bean
   sprouts, chopped cilantro,
   chopped mint

1 In a small bowl, whisk together the gochujang, sesame oil, tamari, ginger, brown sugar, scallions, and ¼ cup water.

2 Soak the mushrooms in the marinade for at least 30 minutes and up to 24 hours.

3 Heat a chargrill on high or a grill pan over high heat, then grill the mushroom caps for 4 minutes or until the sauce is bright red and the mushrooms have nice char marks, rotating and turning them halfway through.

4 Remove the mushrooms from the heat and let cool slightly before slicing into ½-inch strips. Arrange on a serving dish with the remaining vegetables as desired, then serve.

It was on the top floor of the Icon hotel on Kowloon, at the restaurant Above and Beyond, where we had some of the finest modern Chinese cooking in Hong Kong. After our ethereal edamame dumplings with wrappers so thin they literally dissolved on our tongues, we had a Kung Pao tofu dish with whole Kung Pao chiles and toasted cashews. It was so sophisticated and refined, it shamed any goopy rip-off we had ever had back home. When we got back to the States, we started doing Kung Pao everything at Vedge and then at V Street. We have had creamy versions with blended peanut and chunky chile versions as well as the punchy vinaigrette below for flash-fried, chilled string beans. The sauce itself is incredibly versatile and works well on anything, from hot roasted cauliflower to grilled tofu to a grilled and chilled mushroom salad. **SERVES 6 TO 8**

KUNG PAO STRING BEANS

2 tablespoons black vinegar

1 tablespoon sriracha

2 teaspoons pickled chile sauce, optional

2 tablespoons tamari

1 teaspoon chile oil, optional

1 teaspoon sesame oil

2 tablespoons chopped scallions (white parts only)

Canola oil for frying

1 pound string beans (about 3 cups)

½ cup crispy rice noodles, optional

⅛ cup chopped peanuts

1 tablespoon chopped cilantro

1 Combine the black vinegar, sriracha, pickled chile sauce (if using), tamari, chile oil (if using), sesame oil, and scallions in a small bowl. Whisk until well combined (any left over can be kept in the refrigerator for up to 5 days).

2 Line a plate with paper towels. Preheat a fryer to 375°F or heat ½ inch of the oil in a skillet or large saucepan over high heat. Flash-fry the string beans in small batches (about a large handful) just until the skin starts to wrinkle, about 15 seconds, then transfer to the paper towel–lined plate to absorb any excess oil. If you prefer, you may also blanch the beans instead of frying (see Bean Bhajji, page 66).

3 Allow the beans to cool fully before tossing in the dressing, then garnish with the rice noodles (if using), peanuts, and chopped cilantro and serve.

When you think of potatoes, chances are that Ireland will come to mind before Peru. But Peru is where the potato started long before it made its way to Europe. And Papas a la Huancaína is perhaps the best example of a Peruvian signature dish, and it serves as the inspiration for our fries. While the uncommon assembly of garnishes (olives, cilantro, and peanuts) gives the dish its spark, the true star is the aji amarillo sauce, which helps to make these the creamiest, zestiest "loaded" fries you'll ever taste! **SERVES 4**

PERUVIAN FRIES

2 to 3 large Idaho potatoes

Pinch of kosher salt

¼ cup aji amarillo paste (see tip, page 80)

1 teaspoon Dijon mustard

½ cup vegan mayo

½ clove garlic

1 teaspoon chopped shallots

2 teaspoons olive oil

⅛ teaspoon plus an extra pinch of salt

¼ teaspoon freshly ground black pepper

⅛ teaspoon cumin

Canola oil for frying

2 tablespoons chopped roasted, lightly salted peanuts

2 tablespoons chopped black Beldi olives (substitute any oil-cured black olives)

1 tablespoon chopped scallions (green parts only)

1 tablespoon chopped cilantro

1 Preheat the oven to 450°F. Sprinkle the potatoes with a pinch of kosher salt, prick 3 or 4 times with a fork, and wrap each in aluminum foil. Bake until they are cooked thoroughly, about 45 minutes. Remove the potatoes from the oven, discard the foil, and allow the potatoes to cool fully, then slice each potato into 6 long wedges. We prefer to keep the skins on for added flavor and texture.

2 Meanwhile, prepare the sauce by combining the aji amarillo paste with the mustard, mayo, garlic, shallot, olive oil, salt, pepper, and cumin in a blender. Blend until smooth. Leftovers can be stored in the refrigerator for up to 5 days.

3 Line a plate with paper towels. When ready to serve, preheat a fryer to 375°F or heat ½ inch of the oil in a skillet or large saucepan over high heat. Fry the potatoes in the oil until they are golden brown on all sides, about 2 minutes. Remember that the potatoes are already cooked inside, so the outside just needs some color.

(recipe continues)

(recipe continued from previous page)

4 Remove from the oil and transfer to the paper towel–lined plate to absorb any excess oil and sprinkle with the pinch of remaining salt.

5 Transfer to a serving dish and garnish with aji amarillo sauce, peanuts, olives, scallions, and cilantro, then serve.

THREE OTHER USES FOR AJI AMARILLO PASTE

1. Whisk together 1 tablespoon with 1 tablespoon peanut butter, ½ cup sunflower oil, ¼ teaspoon salt, ½ teaspoon black pepper, and 1 tablespoon lime juice to create a tasty and tangy grill marinade.

2. Add 1 tablespoon per cup to salad dressing for a rich, spicy kick.

3. Mix in equal parts with vegan mayo to spread on thick slices of toast and bake, for a Peruvian Welsh rarebit.

It's unfair to judge the humble sweet potato for the clichéd part it plays in Thanksgiving celebrations (in the forms of sticky, sweet pies and side dishes). It is actually incredibly versatile and a very popular winter street food in China. In Beijing, you will find it simply roasted with no frills, served whole with a crackly, char-blistered skin. We added an extra Chinese touch with a blast of black vinegar to both complement and contrast with the sweetness of the potato. Try some vegan sour cream too for an extra shot of richness. **SERVES 4**

GRILLED SWEET POTATOES WITH BLACK VINEGAR

4 medium sweet potatoes

½ teaspoon coarse sea salt

½ cup black vinegar

½ teaspoon sea salt

½ teaspoon white pepper

1 teaspoon sugar

1 tablespoon sesame oil

1 Preheat the oven to 450°F.

2 Sprinkle the sweet potatoes with the salt then wrap each individually in foil and bake until just tender, about 45 minutes. Using a towel, pinch the width of the potatoes to check for doneness. You want them to give a little without being mushy.

3 Whisk together the black vinegar, salt, white pepper, and sugar in a small bowl, then set aside.

4 Preheat a chargill or grill pan to high heat. Remove the potatoes from the foil, cut them into large wedges, then brush them with the sesame oil. Grill potato wedges until you see nice char marks, about 2 minutes.

5 Arrange on serving dishes and drizzle with the black vinegar sauce.

Philadelphians love a good brunch. And we're proud to say that our V Street brunch menu is a perfect balance between the savory plates you'll find on our regular lunch and dinner menus and a few more traditional "brunchy" indulgences. We do tasty waffles (with sesame butter, blackberry preserves, and maple ponzu), a killer Korean Bloody Mary (with kimchi juice!), and a great scrambled poha rice dish (page 112) complete with crunchy papadums (page 41).

These home fries were developed with our brunch menu in mind, and they're sure to start your weekend morning with a blast of flavor. For another twist, take the ingredients from our Peruvian Fries (page 79) and use them to make Peruvian home fries with the potato method here. **SERVES 4 TO 6**

TOGARASHI HOME FRIES

3 Idaho potatoes

Pinch of kosher salt

2 tablespoons gochujang

¼ cup vegan mayo

2 tablespoons sriracha

1 tablespoon sunflower oil

½ cup thinly sliced onion

½ cup diced green bell pepper

2 tablespoons chopped scallions (green parts only)

2 tablespoons chopped cilantro

1 tablespoon Togarashi (page 201)

1 Preheat the oven to 450°F. Sprinkle the potatoes with kosher salt, prick 3 or 4 times, and wrap in aluminum foil. Bake until the potatoes are cooked thoroughly, about 45 minutes. Remove the potatoes from the oven, discard the foil, and allow the potatoes to cool fully, then slice into thin wheels, about ⅛ inch thick.

2 Meanwhile, combine the gochujang, mayo, and sriracha in a medium bowl. Whisk together until smooth. Leftovers can be stored in the refrigerator for up to 5 days.

3 Heat the sunflower oil in a large sauté pan or skillet over high heat until it begins to ripple. Add the onion and bell pepper and sear for 2 minutes. Add the potatoes and sear on all sides, stirring occasionally, until golden brown, about 4 minutes.

4 Transfer the potatoes to a serving dish. Top with the gochujang mayo, scallions, cilantro, and togarashi.

With all the attention on fermented foods these days, you would think they're a passing fad. But back before refrigeration, everyone had to figure out a way to get along after harvest. Smoking and pickling (and eventually canning) became omnipresent. Plus, fermenting techniques carry with them nutritional benefits in addition to great flavor boosts. The longer you ferment, the funkier the flavor. The uses are endless: eat it solo, put it in a stir-fry, make a stew, or churn it into a chunky mayo to serve with fries (see tip, below). This recipe is fairly mild and very versatile. It's great for folks who shy away from the high-test stuff at the Korean market. **MAKES 2 QUARTS**

V STREET KIMCHI

½ cup sea salt

1 cup julienned daikon

3 cups chopped napa cabbage

½ cup thinly sliced onion

3 garlic cloves, peeled and smashed

2 teaspoons minced ginger

1 tablespoon tamari

1 tablespoon gochugaru (Korean chile flakes)

2 tablespoons gochujang

2 teaspoons rice wine vinegar

⅛ teaspoon white pepper

1 teaspoon sesame oil

1 Fill a large bowl or other vessel with 8 cups water, add the salt, and stir to dissolve. Add the daikon, cabbage, and onion and let soak in the salt water for 1 hour. Drain the vegetables in a colander, pressing to release as much water as possible.

2 Whisk together all of the remaining ingredients in a medium bowl.

3 Toss the vegetables in the marinade, massaging it into all the crevices of the cabbage, then pack into an airtight sterilized container, seal, and leave in a dark, cool place for 24 hours to help initiate fermentation. Move the container to a refrigerator and store for an additional 5 days, jostling the container each day to ensure that all vegetables are submerged in marinade. At this point, your kimchi should be ready to go, and the flavor will grow stronger over time. It will keep in your fridge for 2 weeks.

––––––

To whip up some kimchi mayo, combine ½ cup kimchi (strained) plus 2 cups vegan mayo and ½ teaspoon salt. Store in the fridge for up to 3 days.

As great as it is to travel the world to experience new street food, sometimes the best inspiration is right in your own backyard. Here in the United States, we have some of the most delicious corn growing through a decent chunk of the year, and we love to showcase it on our menus when it's at its peak. Blanching and then grilling the corn is the perfect way to prep it for this zesty Israeli interpretation that shows up on our menu in warm weather. Instead of slathering it with butter, we're recommending some spicy Israeli zhoug—an incredibly flavorful Middle Eastern green sauce with a texture between pesto and classic Mexican salsa verde. If you are missing a little extra fat, try mixing the zhoug with some vegan butter. **SERVES 6 TO 8**

ZA'ATAR-GRILLED CORN WITH ZHOUG

ZA'ATAR MARINADE

½ cup sunflower oil

1 teaspoon sherry vinegar

2 tablespoons Za'atar (page 208)

ZHOUG

3 jalapeño peppers, stems and
    seeds removed

¼ cup chopped white onion

1 cup chopped cilantro

½ cup parsley

1 teaspoon cumin

⅛ teaspoon cardamom

2 peeled garlic cloves

1 cup cherry tomatoes, chopped

⅓ cup sunflower oil

1 tablespoon rice wine vinegar

1 teaspoon sea salt

½ teaspoon freshly ground
    black pepper

4 to 8 ears of corn, shucked

1 Combine all of the marinade ingredients in a blender and blend until smooth. Leftovers can be stored in the refrigerator for up to 7 days.

2 Combine all of the zhoug ingredients in a food processor and process until the peppers and herbs are broken down and the mixture is the consistency of a loose pesto. Leftovers can be stored in the refrigerator for up to 4 days.

3 Bring a large pot of salted water to a rolling boil over high heat. Blanch the corn for 8 minutes, then drain.

4 Preheat a chargrill to high or a grill pan over high heat, then brush each ear with about 2 tablespoons of za'atar marinade. Grill the corn briefly until lightly charred.

5 Top the corn with zhoug and serve immediately.

We've created some interesting ways to serve greens over the years and we pride ourselves on keeping things exciting. One of our best sources for inspiration is a trip to any of the vibrant Asian markets we have here in Philadelphia. The produce departments are always overflowing with the freshest and most exotic vegetables. It's hard to keep them all straight, but we've chosen our favorites to use in this recipe. Most people recognize bok choy, but look out for yu choy, which has a thick stem and flat leaves, as well as Chinese broccoli, which has an even thicker base and flower shoots like broccoli rabe. A quick blanch, a little sesame action, and some funky turnips are just the trick to transform "eating your greens" from a chore to an exciting culinary experience. **SERVES 6**

MARKET GREENS WITH PICKLED TURNIPS

4 cups white vinegar

⅓ cup sugar

3 tablespoons plus ¼ teaspoon sea salt

2 cups diced turnips

One 4- to 6-ounce piece of ginger cut in half, unpeeled (will be discarded)

2 bunches baby bok choy

2 bunches yu choy

2 bunches Chinese broccoli

1 tablespoon sunflower oil

2 teaspoons minced garlic

¼ teaspoon freshly ground black pepper

Sesame seeds and chopped scallions (green parts only) for garnish

1 Whisk together ¼ cup water, the vinegar, sugar, and 3 tablespoons of the salt in a medium stockpot to form a brine. Add the turnips and ginger to brine and bring to a boil over medium heat. Boil for 3 minutes or until tender.

2 Drain the vegetables, discarding the ginger. Set the turnips aside.

3 Bring a large pot of water to a rolling boil over high heat and prepare an ice water bath (approximately 4 quarts cold water with 1 quart ice).

4 Meanwhile, chop the baby bok choy into 1-inch-long pieces and chop the other greens into 2-inch-long pieces.

(recipe continues)

(recipe continued from previous page)

5 Blanch the boy choy first by submerging it in the boiling water for 30 seconds, then removing it and dunking it immediately into the ice water bath.

6 Repeat the blanching process with the other greens, this time for just 10 seconds each, and add them to the ice water bath. Drain all greens from the ice water.

7 Heat the sunflower oil in a large sauté pan over high heat. When the oil begins to ripple, add the garlic, then the greens, sprinkle with the remaining salt and pepper, and cook for 2 minutes. Stir occasionally and cook until all greens are seared evenly, about 1 more minute.

8 Transfer the greens to a serving dish, top with the pickled turnips, and garnish with the sesame seeds and chopped scallions.

THE TOFU TRAIL

Tofu has to be one of the easiest foods to slide onto a stick, making it incredibly street food–friendly. It used to be the evil icon of a plant-based diet, but we're changing all that. We've come to appreciate the genius moment when someone first came up with the idea to make cheese from soy beans, we understand its long, wonderful history, and we've learned how best to cook it. And when we travel we seek it out everywhere.

On the Thai island of Phuket, we found "hard tofu stew" seared and shined with a dark sauce tingling with ginger, chile, and lime. Its deep, layered stew of aromatics was an unfolding trip through Southeast Asian cooking.

In Singapore, we found the most extreme stinky tofu yet, almost still sizzling in fermentation, creamy as cream cheese, yet with a funk to end all funks, served as a topping for congee.

On the island of St. Lucia, at a Caribbean barbecue where we thought there would be nothing for us to eat, there were tofu kebabs slicked with a jerk marinade and a little Scotch bonnet kick. A perfect match for the lush setting at water's edge with glasses of Bounty Rum on ice.

On the Big Island of Hawaii (Kona) there was a straight-up tofu steak on a restaurant menu. A "steak" is a cut not exclusive to meat, but exclusive to cooking. It evokes satisfaction, knife-and-fork work, and dispels the notion that plant-based food has to be all chopped up into a stew or stir-fry. This tofu came out with grill marks and bronzed with a soy-ginger lacquer, surrounded by a garden of baby vegetables—a classic protein-starch-veg meal that was at once both exotic and familiar.

Our vision for the future of tofu is right in the center of New American cuisine. If you understand and respect it, tofu's a chef's dream ingredient. It's a blank canvas on which to paint any flavor, from any cuisine. More American chefs are getting their hands on it and not letting go. Its potential is endless.

PLATES

Carrot Choripan 94

Bocadillos 97

Huli Huli Barbecue
Seitan Tacos 99

Korean Fried Tempeh Tacos 101

Black Garlic Pierogi 102

West Indian Socca with
Hearts of Palm and Avocado 104

Langos 106

Trumpet Mushroom
Shawarma 109

Afghani Bolani 110

Scrambled Poha Rice 112

Doubles Bara Bread 114

Eggplant Sabich 117

Pho French Dip 119

A choripan is Argentina's answer to the hot dog, traditionally done with sausage and topped with, well, everything. It's a street food classic that we have our own take on with Carrot Asado (page 70) in place of the meat and a homemade potato roll. The carrots are smoky and succulent, and when paired with this light and fluffy bun, they create an amazingly satisfying "hot dog" just begging to be loaded up with black bean puree and curtido slaw. Why stop there? Add some avocado, hot sauce, onions, and pickles—you know, the works! **SERVES 6**

CARROT CHORIPAN

¼ cup diced, peeled Baker's potato

2 teaspoons agave syrup

¾ teaspoon active dry yeast

2 tablespoons vegan butter

¾ teaspoon sea salt

1 teaspoon egg replacer powder

1½ cups all-purpose flour plus more for dusting

1 teaspoon plus 1 tablespoon sunflower oil

1 teaspoon minced garlic

2 tablespoons diced onion

2 tablespoons diced green bell pepper

½ teaspoon light brown sugar

1 teaspoon Latin Spice Blend (page 210)

¾ teaspoon cumin

1 tablespoon ketchup

½ teaspoon molasses

⅔ cup vegetable stock

One 15.5-ounce can black beans, drained and rinsed

1 Begin by making the potato rolls. Line a sheet pan with parchment paper and set aside. Poke holes in the potato with a fork, microwave on high for 1 to 5 minutes, or until fully tender, then mash with a fork. Transfer to a medium bowl and stir together with the agave, yeast, and 2 tablespoons water. Let sit for 5 minutes to allow the yeast to activate, then add the butter, ¼ teaspoon of the salt, egg replacer, and flour. Knead for 4 minutes, until the dough forms a small ball. Place in a lightly greased bowl and cover with a clean kitchen towel, then set in a warm place to proof for 1 hour or until it doubles in size.

2 While the dough is rising, make the black bean puree. Heat 1 teaspoon of the sunflower oil in a large sauté pan over medium heat. Add the garlic, onion, and green pepper and sauté until the onion and garlic caramelize and are golden brown, about 3 minutes. Add ¼ teaspoon of the salt, the brown sugar, Latin Spice Blend, ½ teaspoon of the cumin, the ketchup, molasses, and vegetable stock. Stir until all the ingredients are well combined, then reduce the heat to low and simmer until the onions

(recipe continues)

(recipe continued from previous page)

1 teaspoon lemon juice

1 teaspoon sherry vinegar

1 teaspoon Dijon mustard

½ teaspoon freshly ground
    black pepper

2 tablespoons sliced scallions
    (green parts only)

1 cup thinly sliced white cabbage

¼ cup chopped cilantro

¼ cup slivered red onion

Carrot Asado (page 70)

Sliced avocado, hot sauce, diced
    onions, and sliced pickles,
    optional

start to become translucent, about 5 minutes. Remove from the heat and cool fully. Transfer to a food processor, add the black beans, and pulse until smooth and creamy, about 3 minutes. (Leftovers can be stored in the refrigerator for up to 3 days.)

3 Whisk together the lemon juice, vinegar, mustard, remaining sunflower oil, remaining salt, pepper, and remaining cumin in a large bowl to make the dressing for the curtido. Toss the scallions, cabbage, cilantro, and red onion in the dressing until they are evenly coated. Transfer the curtido to an airtight container and store in the refrigerator for at least 30 minutes before serving.

4 Preheat the oven to 400°F. Return to the potato rolls by transferring the dough from the bowl to a lightly floured work surface. Cut it into 6 balls and form each into a 6-inch-long cylinder. Transfer to the prepared sheet pan and let sit, uncovered, for 15 minutes. Bake the rolls for 10 minutes, or until they are golden brown, rotating the sheet pan halfway through.

5 Remove the rolls from the oven and let cool slightly before slicing and stuffing with the black bean puree, Carrot Asado, and curtido. Garnish with additional toppings as desired and serve.

While connecting through Madrid we stumbled upon this crazy pop-up restaurant in our hotel where a few chefs from Seville were running some incredibly creative dishes that honored the tapas tradition, like potato shaved into noodles and served in a Chinese takeout container with both Spanish and Asian spices. This bocadillo is essentially a Spanish hoagie stuffed with tapas-inspired ingredients. This one dish is all you will need for lunch. **MAKES 2 HOAGIES, SERVES 6**

BOCADILLOS

2 red bell peppers

2 tablespoons olive oil plus extra for finishing

2 teaspoons sherry vinegar

1 teaspoon sea salt plus extra for the potato and tomatoes

1 teaspoon freshly ground black pepper

1 teaspoon crushed garlic

1 teaspoon Old Bay seasoning

2 teaspoons smoked paprika

²/₃ cup vegan mayo

1 large potato, baked

1 tablespoon sunflower (or neutral) oil

2 hoagie (sub) rolls or a baguette, split in half

6 tomato slices

8 ounces packaged sliced smoked tofu

1 cup chopped spinach

Red onion slices

¼ cup chopped green olives

2 tablespoons capers

1 Char the outsides of the red bell peppers on a stovetop burner set to medium-high heat. Turn with tongs. Once cool, remove as much skin as possible with a clean kitchen towel and cut into ½-inch-thin strips.

2 Dress the peppers with 1 tablespoon of the olive oil, 1 teaspoon of the sherry vinegar, ½ teaspoon salt, ½ teaspoon of the black pepper, and the garlic.

3 Combine the remaining 1 tablespoon olive oil, remaining 1 teaspoon vinegar, remaining ½ teaspoon salt, remaining ½ teaspoon pepper, the Old Bay, smoked paprika, and mayo in a medium bowl.

4 Cut the potato into 1-inch cubes. Heat the sunflower oil in a large sauté pan over high heat until it starts to ripple.

5 Pan-fry the potato cubes, turning with a spoon until they are evenly browned, 3 to 5 minutes. Remove to a paper towel and sprinkle with salt.

6 To assemble the bocadillos, layer each roll in the following order: 2 tablespoons of mayo, tomatoes (sprinkled with a little salt), potatoes, smoked tofu, roasted peppers, spinach, onions, olives, and capers. Drizzle with additional olive oil and enjoy.

Over the years, we've grown quite the reputation for our seitan. We work with a local producer to create some of the region's tastiest, most tender seitan, and we showcase it in several different preparations. At our sister restaurant Vedge, one of our favorite takes is char-grilled seitan with za'atar spice over creamy tahini with grilled black kale and pickled turnips. We've also shredded it, braised it with cabbage and gochujang, and served it with kimchi mayo (page 85). But our most popular seitan dish to date has to be our barbecue. Seitan takes beautifully to a Hawaiian-inspired Huli Huli barbecue sauce in this recipe that works great hot or chilled. **SERVES 4 TO 6**

HULI HULI BARBECUE SEITAN TACOS

½ cup ketchup

2 teaspoons molasses

2⅓ tablespoons sunflower oil

¼ teaspoon sesame oil

½ teaspoon tamari

½ teaspoon lime juice

1 teaspoon minced ginger

¼ teaspoon cumin

¼ teaspoon freshly ground black pepper

2 tablespoons sriracha

16 ounces seitan

2 tablespoons Latin Spice Blend (page 210)

Six 6-inch tortillas

1 Prepare the Huli Huli barbecue sauce by combining the ketchup, molasses, ⅓ tablespoon of the sunflower oil, sesame oil, tamari, lime juice, ginger, cumin, pepper, and sriracha in a medium bowl. Whisk together until smooth. Transfer to an airtight container and store in the refrigerator for up to 5 days.

2 Next, use your hands to shred the seitan into thick chunks about 2 inches in length. Pulling it apart with your hands allows you to follow the natural break points and create a rustic effect.

3 Toss the seitan in a medium bowl with the remaining sunflower oil and Latin Spice Blend until it's evenly coated.

4 Heat a large sauté pan or skillet over high heat, then sear the seitan a little at a time until the edges are crispy and brown. Slowly add the Huli Huli barbecue sauce until the seitan is evenly coated.

(recipe continues)

(recipe continued from previous page)

Reduce the heat to medium, stirring occasionally, until sauce caramelizes around the seitan, about 2 minutes.

5 Heat the tortillas over the open flame of a range just until toasted, about 30 seconds on each side, or wrapped in foil in a 350°F oven for 10 minutes. Stuff the tortillas with warm barbecue seitan and serve with garnishes of your choice such as Hearts of Palm Slaw (page 55) or Lomi Tomato Salad (page 55).

You can't resist a good taco. Our favorite of the bazillions we've served over the years features crispy tempeh, the Asian fermented soybean cake. It's incredibly filling because it's super high in protein, and its nutty flavor takes really well to all the fun accents like funky kimchi and fiery sriracha. **SERVES 4**

KOREAN FRIED TEMPEH TACOS

1 teaspoon tamari

1 teaspoon sesame oil

1 teaspoon rice wine vinegar

1 sheet kombu, broken in pieces

One 8-ounce plank tempeh, cut into 8 slices

1 cup unsweetened soy milk

½ cup Dijon mustard

½ teaspoon sea salt

½ teaspoon freshly ground black pepper

2 teaspoons Togarashi (page 201)

2⅔ cups chickpea flour or rice flour

¼ cup gochujang

½ cup vegan mayo

2 tablespoons sriracha

Canola oil for frying

Eight 6-inch tortillas

½ cup kimchi (page 85)

2 tablespoons chopped scallions (green parts only)

1 Combine 1 cup water, the tamari, sesame oil, rice wine vinegar, and the kombu in a medium saucepan. Bring to a boil, remove the kombu, and add the tempeh. Cook just until it starts to flake, about 4 minutes. Remove the tempeh from the broth, then set aside to cool.

2 Combine the soy milk, mustard, salt, pepper, togarashi, and ⅓ cup of the flour. Place the remaining rice flour in a separate shallow dish.

3 Whisk together the gochujang, mayo, and sriracha in a separate small bowl. Any leftovers can be stored in the refrigerator for up to 1 week.

4 Line a plate with paper towels. Preheat a fryer to 375°F or heat ½ inch of the oil in a skillet or large saucepan over high heat.

5 Dunk the tempeh in the batter, then dredge in the remaining rice flour. Fry a few pieces at a time until golden brown, about 3 minutes. Transfer to the paper towel–lined plate to absorb any excess oil.

6 Heat the tortillas over the open flame of a range or wrapped in foil in a 350°F oven for 10 minutes. Stuff them with fried tempeh. Top with the gochujang sauce, kimchi, and scallions, and serve.

We have a tradition at our restaurants; you could call it pierogi season. It kicks off around mid-November when Kate makes pierogis at home for the holidays—pierogis that are so delicious you can just picture all her Polish ancestors smiling and reaching for the vegan sour cream! But it also reminds us how well pierogis fit on the menu at V Street. Of course, we jazz them up a bit by adding caramelized onions that have been deglazed with a little black vinegar. And the fermented black garlic amps up the tang in the cool sour cream—a perfect contrast to the hot crispy dough and the indulgently fluffy potato filling. There is simply no better way to welcome in the holidays. **SERVES 6**

BLACK GARLIC PIEROGI

2 cups all-purpose flour plus more for dusting

1 teaspoon sea salt

4 tablespoons (½ stick) vegan butter

2 tablespoons vegan shortening

2 tablespoons olive oil

4 cups peeled, chopped Yukon Gold potato

½ cup plus 2 tablespoons vegan sour cream

2 tablespoons sunflower oil plus more for searing

½ cup diced onion

2 tablespoons minced black garlic (see tip, opposite)

1 tablespoon black vinegar

1 teaspoon tamari

1 teaspoon lemon juice

¼ teaspoon freshly ground black pepper

2 tablespoons chopped scallions (green parts only)

1 Make the dough by pulsing the flour with ½ teaspoon of the salt, 2 tablespoons of the butter, and the shortening in a food processor until the mixture resembles sand. Stream in the olive oil, then slowly add about ¼ cup cold water just until a loose dough forms. Remove the dough from the food processor, form it into a ball, wrap in plastic wrap, and refrigerate for 20 minutes.

2 While the dough is chilling, bring a large stockpot full of salted water to a boil over high heat. Boil the potatoes for about 10 minutes, or until they become tender. Drain and cool for 10 minutes before transferring to a large bowl. Mash with the remaining ½ teaspoon salt, remaining 2 tablespoons butter, and 2 tablespoons of the sour cream and set aside.

3 Heat the sunflower oil in a large sauté pan over medium heat. Sauté the onion and 1 tablespoon of the black garlic just until the onion becomes translucent, stirring occasionally, about 5 minutes. Deglaze by adding the black vinegar and tamari and stirring, scraping up any browned bits that may have stuck to the pan. Add to the potatoes and mash together.

4 Whisk together the remaining ½ cup sour cream in a small bowl with the remaining 1 tablespoon black garlic, lemon juice, pepper, and chopped scallions. If making ahead, transfer the mixture to an airtight container and store in the refrigerator for up to 2 days.

5 On a lightly floured work surface, roll out the dough to ¼ inch thick and cut out 4-inch round circles. Stuff each circle with 1½ tablespoons of the potato mixture, fold in half, and seal by crimping with your fingers or a fork. Repeat until all the dough is used (about 18 pierogis).

6 Bring a large pot of salted water to a boil. Boil the pierogis, four to six at a time, until they rise to the surface of the water and the dough is tender, about 3 minutes. Allow them to cool for a few minutes. Add a shallow layer of sunflower oil to a large sauté pan or skillet over high heat. Sear the pierogis on each side until golden brown, about 2 minutes. Serve immediately with black garlic sour cream.

THREE OTHER USES FOR BLACK GARLIC

1. Throw some in your next batch of kimchi (1 tablespoon per quart) for a little extra funk.

2. Whip it with vegan mayo (1 tablespoon per cup) for a nouveau French onion dip!

3. Mix 1 cup vegan mayo with ¼ cup mustard, 1 teaspoon capers, 1 teaspoon lemon juice, and 1 teaspoon minced garlic for a new take on Caesar dressing.

Southern French cooking, as in Provençal and the Mediterranean, is a world away from what most people consider classic French food. Gone are the butters and heavy creams—it's all about olive oil and tomatoes in the southern part of the country. In Nice, dry garbanzo beans are used to create a flour that becomes the base for a standout southern French–style pancake. A great naturally gluten-free alternative to Brittany's savory and sweet crepes, socca make for a wonderful canvas for all kinds of fillings and sauces. In this recipe we took inspiration from a recent trip to Martinique, an island that's about as French as they come, and landed this dish deep in the French Caribbean, topping it with hearts of palm and avocado and sneaking in a touch of jerk sauce. **SERVES 4**

WEST INDIAN SOCCA WITH HEARTS OF PALM AND AVOCADO

¼ cup vegan mayo

1 teaspoon Dijon mustard

½ teaspoon Jerk Sauce (page 206)

2 teaspoons ketchup

½ teaspoon curry powder

½ teaspoon sea salt

1½ cups shredded hearts of palm

¼ cup diced red bell pepper

2 tablespoons chopped scallions (white parts only)

1 cup chopped avocado

SOCCA

1 cup chickpea flour

¼ teaspoon curry powder

½ teaspoon sea salt

¼ teaspoon coriander

¼ teaspoon cumin

1 teaspoon olive oil plus more for searing

1 Whisk together the mayo, Dijon mustard, jerk sauce, ketchup, curry powder, and salt in a large bowl. Add the hearts of palm, red bell pepper, scallions, and avocado and toss gently until all the vegetables are evenly dressed. If making ahead, transfer to an airtight container and store in the refrigerator for up to 3 days.

2 Sift the chickpea flour together with the curry powder, salt, coriander, and cumin in a medium bowl. Whisk in 1 cup water and 1 teaspoon of the olive oil. Transfer to an airtight container and chill in the refrigerator for 1 hour and up to 24 hours.

3 Preheat the oven to the lowest setting. Heat a large sauté pan over medium-high heat. Coat the bottom of the pan with 1 teaspoon of the olive oil, then ladle in ¼ cup of the socca batter and swirl it around to create a very thin pancake. Cook until bubbles start to form in the center, 1½ minutes, then flip and cook on the other side just until it browns, 1 additional minute. Remove the socca and keep on a sheet pan covered with foil, in the oven. Repeat with the remaining batter, using just enough olive oil to lightly coat the bottom of the pan for each pancake as needed.

4 When ready to serve, lay the pancakes flat and place $1/2$ cup of the hearts of palm salad in the center, then roll up in a tube shape and arrange on a serving plate.

On the streets of Budapest, you will undoubtedly find people walking around enjoying langos, one of the tastiest street snacks imaginable. You could describe a lango as a savory potato donut, but that doesn't quite do it justice. It actually looks like a little personal pizza, all puffy and golden brown on the edges, then topped with all sorts of rich, indulgent spreads and accoutrements. Traditionally, Hungarians slather them with sour cream, cheese, and ham. Our version is topped with a tangy sauerkraut remoulade and bits of smoked Chioggia beets, then generously sprinkled with fresh chopped dill and cracked black pepper. No doubt the dough takes practice, but once you get it down, this is the ultimate comfort food. **SERVES 6 TO 8**

LANGOS

1½ tablespoons active dry yeast

½ cup unsweetened soy milk, warmed

2¼ teaspoons sugar

1 teaspoon sunflower oil

1 Idaho potato, baked, peeled, and mashed

1¼ cups all-purpose flour plus more for dusting

¼ teaspoon sea salt

4 medium Chioggia beets (substitute golden beets; see page 108)

1 teaspoon Montreal steak seasoning

1 teaspoon sherry vinegar

⅓ cup sauerkraut

1 tablespoon capers

2 tablespoons chopped red onion

½ teaspoon minced garlic

2 tablespoons chopped dill, plus more for garnish, optional

1 tablespoon chopped chives

1 Combine the yeast, soy milk, and sugar in a small bowl. Set aside for 10 minutes, until the yeast has fully activated; you will see lots of bubbles at the surface.

2 Line a sheet pan with parchment paper and set aside. Coat a large bowl with ¼ teaspoon of the sunflower oil, then add the mashed potato, flour, and salt, and stir to combine. Add the yeast mixture and mix until a soft dough forms. Transfer to a lightly floured work surface and knead for 5 minutes, until the dough ball becomes firm. If you prefer to use an electric mixer, use a J-shaped dough hook and knead for 5 minutes. Transfer the dough ball to a lightly greased bowl and cover with a clean kitchen towel, then set aside in a warm place to proof for 1 hour.

3 Bring a large pot of salted water to a boil over high heat. Boil the beets just until tender, about 45 minutes. Drain and set aside until cool enough to handle. Peel and slice the beets into ⅛-inch wheels.

(recipe continues)

(recipe continued from previous page)

½ cup vegan mayo

1½ tablespoons Dijon mustard

½ teaspoon freshly ground black pepper, plus more for serving, optional

Canola oil for frying

4 Toss the beets with the remaining ³⁄₄ teaspoon sunflower oil, Montreal seasoning, and sherry vinegar in a medium bowl. Heat a medium sauté pan over high heat, add the beets, and sauté until the edges are golden brown, about 5 minutes. Remove from heat and let cool fully, then chop the beets into a rough dice. If making ahead, transfer to an airtight container and store in the refrigerator for up to 5 days.

5 Combine the sauerkraut, capers, red onion, garlic, dill, chives, mayo, mustard, and pepper in a food processor. Pulse until just combined and the mixture is creamy but chunky. Transfer to an airtight container and store in the refrigerator for up to 1 week.

6 Transfer the dough to a lightly floured work surface and cut into four even pieces. Shape each piece into a 4-inch circle, transfer to the prepared sheet pan, and let rise, uncovered, for 20 minutes.

7 Line a plate with paper towels. Preheat a fryer to 375°F or heat a shallow layer of the canola oil in a large sauté pan over high heat. Fry the langos until golden brown on both sides, about 4 minutes total, flipping after 2 minutes. Transfer to the paper towel–lined plate to absorb any excess oil. Top with the remoulade and beets, garnish with additional dill and cracked pepper, if desired, and serve.

For extra flavor, smoke the beets in a smoker box with applewood chips for 2 minutes.

How can you make shawarma out of mushrooms? It's easy. You can make shawarma out of anything; it's one of those dishes that people wrongfully associate only with meat. We find that toothsome, juicy trumpet mushrooms take amazingly well to a good sear and those aromatic Middle Eastern spices. Stuff them into a homemade pita with a creamy, tangy sauce or hummus, and you have an amazing Middle Eastern sandwich that is less about the protein and all about authentic flavor. **SERVES 4 TO 6**

TRUMPET MUSHROOM SHAWARMA

1 cup cooked chickpeas

1 teaspoon salt

½ teaspoon freshly ground black pepper

1 garlic clove

3 tablespoons tahini

1 tablespoon lemon juice

⅓ cup olive oil

4 cups trumpet mushrooms, sliced thin (substitute oysters or portobellos)

1 teaspoon plus 1 tablespoon sunflower oil

1 tablespoon Latin Spice Blend (page 210)

2 teaspoons Za'atar (page 208)

1 teaspoon curry powder

6 House Pitas (page 32)

Shredded lettuce

Tomato slices

Onion slices

Hot peppers

1 Combine the chickpeas, salt, pepper, garlic, tahini, and lemon juice in a food processor and pulse until smooth, drizzling in ¼ cup warm water and the olive oil as you pulse. The warm water keeps the chickpeas tender. Any leftovers can be stored in the refrigerator for up to 3 days.

2 Toss the sliced trumpet mushrooms in a large bowl with 1 teaspoon of the sunflower oil, the Latin Spice Blend, za'atar, and curry powder until the mushrooms are evenly coated. Heat a large sauté pan or skillet over high heat with the remaining 1 tablespoon sunflower oil and sear the mushrooms in small batches until crispy, about 2 minutes.

3 When ready to serve, slice the side of each pita to create a pocket. Spread the hummus inside, then stuff with mushrooms. Add shredded lettuce, tomato, onion, hot peppers, and any other toppings—such as our Pickled Turnips (page 89), Harissa (page 74), or Zhoug (page 86)—then serve.

Not sure if we'll ever make it to Afghanistan. But that doesn't stop us from taking an interest in the culture. Bolani is a delicious stuffed flatbread that you'll find served for special occasions in Afghanistan, traditionally filled with any combination of leeks, spinach, lentils, potatoes, or pumpkin, as we're highlighting here. While frying is traditional, most Western kebab houses have taken to baking the flatbreads not only to cut back on fat but also to keep the bread billowy and light. **SERVES 8**

AFGHANI BOLANI

3½ cups flour

1 teaspoon salt

1 teaspoon plus 1 tablespoon olive oil, plus more if baking

2 cups peeled, cubed pumpkin (substitute calabaza or acorn squash)

1 cup thinly chopped leeks

¼ teaspoon freshly ground black pepper

¼ teaspoon coriander

4 cups spinach

1 cup mashed potato

1 tablespoon chopped cilantro

Sunflower oil for pan frying

1 Lightly oil a large bowl. Sift together the flour and ½ teaspoon of the salt in a large bowl. Slowly add 1⅓ cups warm water and 1 teaspoon of olive oil, then mix until a tight, elastic dough forms, about 5 minutes. Form the dough into a ball, set it aside in the lightly greased bowl, then cover with a clean kitchen towel and let rest in a warm place for 1 hour.

2 Cut the dough into 8 even parts and form each into a ball. Set aside on a parchment-lined sheet pan and let rest for an additional 20 minutes.

3 Preheat the oven to 400°F. Start the filling by tossing the pumpkin and leeks with the remaining ½ teaspoon salt, remaining 1 tablespoon olive oil, the pepper, and coriander. Transfer to a sheet pan and roast until the pumpkin is tender and the leeks begin to caramelize, about 20 minutes. Remove from the oven and toss with the spinach, allowing the heat to lightly wilt the spinach. Then fold in the mashed potato and cilantro. Leave the oven on if you prefer to bake rather than pan-fry the bolani.

4 Roll each dough ball into a ¼-inch oval shape. Arrange about ⅓ cup filling on half the dough, leaving a ½-inch border at the edges so you can crimp. Fold the dough over the filling and crimp the edges shut with a fork. Gently lift the stuffed dough, stretching it a bit.

5 Line a plate with paper towels. Heat a large skillet with a shallow layer of oil on high heat until it ripples. Gently place the bolani into the sunflower oil and pan-fry until golden and crispy, about 2 minutes on each side. If you prefer to bake the bolani, simply arrange them on a parchment-lined sheet pan, brush lightly on each side with olive oil, and bake for about 18 minutes at 400°F, until puffy and golden brown.

6 Transfer to the paper towel–lined plate to absorb any excess oil and serve immediately.

India is famous for its basmati rice, but poha from western central India is where things get really interesting. Raw rice grains are flattened into little flakes that require a bit of water to rehydrate them for use in salads or porridge. We find the texture to be somewhere between a risotto and scrambled eggs. In this curry-spiced scrambled tofu, turmeric gives a nice golden color to the tofu, and the fresh herbs and tomato chutney make this a bright and spicy way to start your day. **SERVES 2**

SCRAMBLED POHA RICE

1 cup chopped tomato

2 tablespoons cilantro leaves

2 tablespoons plus ½ cup finely diced red onion

¼ teaspoon minced ginger

¼ teaspoon minced garlic

1 tablespoon ketchup

1 tablespoon sriracha

½ tablespoon olive oil

2 teaspoons curry powder

½ teaspoon cumin

¼ teaspoon cayenne pepper

1½ teaspoons sea salt

1 cup poha

8 ounces firm tofu

⅛ teaspoon turmeric

1 cup vegetable stock

¼ teaspoon freshly ground black pepper

½ teaspoon Latin Spice Blend (page 210)

1 teaspoon nutritional yeast

1 tablespoon sunflower oil

1 teaspoon cumin seeds

1 tablespoon vegan butter

1 Start by making the tomato chutney. Combine the tomato, cilantro, 2 tablespoons of the red onion, ginger, garlic, ketchup, sriracha, olive oil, ½ teaspoon of the curry powder, cumin, cayenne, and ¾ teaspoon of the salt in a food processor. Pulse until the herbs are lightly torn, about 30 seconds. Any leftovers can be stored in the refrigerator for up to 3 days.

2 Next, rehydrate the poha by soaking it in a medium bowl with 1 cup warm water until the rice is softened and fluffy, about 2 minutes. Drain off any remaining water.

3 In a separate medium bowl, mash together the tofu with 1 teaspoon of the curry powder, the remaining ¾ teaspoon salt, and the turmeric.

4 Whisk together the vegetable stock with the remaining ½ teaspoon curry powder, the pepper, Latin Spice Blend, and the nutritional yeast in a small bowl.

5 Heat the sunflower oil in a large sauté pan over high heat, add the remaining ½ cup red onion, and the cumin seeds. Cook until the onions are translucent, about 2 minutes. Add the tofu mixture, stirring occasionally, until the tofu is yellow throughout with areas of golden brown, about 5 minutes.

6 Add the vegan butter and let it melt, then add the poha and continue cooking until warmed all the way through, about 3 minutes.

7 Add the vegetable stock mixture and bring to a boil, scraping up any browned bits stuck to the pan. Stir to combine the poha mixture, then transfer to serving dishes. Garnish with the tomato chutney and serve.

You just have to love Trinidad, home to steel drums and the strongest Indian influence of any Caribbean island. Combine that with a rich culture and the indigenous Caribbean spices and you have yourself some mind-blowing street food complete with an awesome soundtrack! Doubles is a national obsession and naturally vegan. It's a thick, spiced chickpea stew that goes in or on bara bread, which is a cumin-scented puffy wheat bread loosely related to roti or naan. A brunch staple at V Street, bara bread is served on top of a bowl of our Spicy Chana Stew (page 131) with scrambled tofu. We garnish it with avocado and cilantro but that's where you can get creative. Try the Escoveitch Cabbage (page 63) or diced fresh tomatoes or mango. One thing that's essential on ours is a nice shot of V Street hot sauce (page 204)! **MAKES 12 BARA**

DOUBLES BARA BREAD

2 teaspoons active dry yeast

2 teaspoons sugar

2 cups all-purpose flour plus more for dusting

½ teaspoon crushed toasted cumin seeds (toasted in a dry pan and then crushed/chopped with a knife)

½ teaspoon sea salt

1 teaspoon turmeric powder

⅛ cup diced chives

½ teaspoon white pepper

¼ cup sunflower oil

Canola oil for frying

1 Combine ¾ cup warm water, the yeast, and sugar in a medium bowl. Allow to sit for 5 minutes, until the yeast blooms.

2 While the yeast is blooming, combine the flour, cumin, salt, turmeric, chives, and pepper in a large bowl.

3 Add the yeast mixture to the dry ingredients along with the sunflower oil. Mix with a spoon, adding water 1 tablespoon at a time, up to ¼ cup if needed, just until the dough forms a soft, sticky ball.

4 Transfer the dough to a lightly floured surface and knead by hand to further incorporate the dough, about 5 minutes. Place back in the bowl, cover with a clean kitchen towel, and set aside to proof for 1 hour.

5 Divide the dough into 12 equal portions, about the size of a golf ball. An easy way to do this is to cut the dough in half, then into 3 equal portions, and then cut each section in half again. Roll the dough into tight balls. Let rest, uncovered, for at least 20 minutes on a clean surface, then flatten into disks.

6 Line plates with paper towels or have ready a wire cooling rack. Heat about 3 inches of canola oil in a deep frying pan over medium-high heat until it ripples. When the oil is ready, fry the baras until puffed and golden, 15 to 30 seconds on each side. Drain on paper towels or a wire rack.

Sabich is the poor cousin of falafel. Much less known but just as delicious, it features grilled or fried eggplant with hard-boiled egg, hummus, or tahini and an Israeli salad. Sabich varies from region to region and from chef to chef, but is always based around the eggplant. The beauty of this sandwich is that once you have the pita and the eggplant, you can take complete culinary freedom by adding nearly any of the Middle Eastern recipes in this book such as the Chermoula Hummus (page 32), Pickled Turnips (page 89), and the Harissa-Grilled Cauliflower (page 74). Remember to buy the freshest eggplant possible. It should have very shiny, unblemished skin and the flesh should be white. Eggplant is one vegetable that is almost impossible to "fix" once it has started to go so don't mess around with an old eggplant, it just won't work. **SERVES 4**

EGGPLANT SABICH

1 cup sunflower oil

¼ cup ketchup

1 tablespoon sherry vinegar

1 tablespoon minced garlic

2 tablespoons tamari

2 tablespoons Za'atar (page 208)

1 teaspoon sea salt

3 Chinese eggplants, tops removed and halved lengthwise

4 House Pitas (page 32)

1 Whisk together the oil, ketchup, sherry vinegar, minced garlic, tamari, za'atar, and salt in a small bowl.

2 Heat a chargrill on high or a grill pan over high heat. Brush the eggplant halves with the marinade before placing on the grill, flesh side down. Grill until they are soft and begin to char, about 5 minutes. Turn over to blister the skin on the other side, about 2 minutes. Remove from the grill and allow to cool.

3 Cut the eggplants on a bias to create 1-inch spears then set aside.

4 On each of the 4 pitas, spread Chermoula Hummus (page 32), a drizzle of Harissa (page 74), a tablespoon of Pickled Turnips (page 89), and a sprinkle of za'atar (page 208; about 1 teaspoon per pita). Top with your choice of vegetables, lettuce, tomato, onion, pickles, hot peppers, and other toppings.

The French influence in Vietnam persists today in Vietnamese communities all over the world. Here in Philadelphia, you'll see markets with spicy chili sauces and bamboo shoots next to aisles of freshly baked baguettes and pastries. We celebrate this fusion on our brunch menu by combining all the fresh herbs and spices from a traditional bahn mi with the fun dipping action of a classic French dip sandwich. Using both shiitake and oyster mushrooms, we coax a rich, unctuous flavor for our pho-inspired jus, but you can build the sandwich itself with tofu, seitan, or even vegan sausage. A little sambal oelek on the side is a must, so roll up your sleeves and enjoy! **SERVES 2**

PHO FRENCH DIP

2 tablespoons black vinegar

2 teaspoons five-spice powder

1 tablespoon sesame oil

¼ teaspoon white pepper

½ teaspoon minced garlic

½ teaspoon minced ginger

¼ teaspoon sea salt

2 tablespoons sunflower oil

2 cups trimmed oyster mushrooms (substitute chanterelles or buttons)

2 cups shiitake mushroom caps

2 cups Pho Broth (page 120)

1 tablespoon vegan mayo

1 tablespoon sriracha

1 medium baguette, sliced lengthwise and then crosswise

¼ cup chopped basil

1 tablespoon chopped scallions (green parts only)

1 tablespoon chopped cilantro

1 tablespoon jalapeño slices (optional)

1 Whisk together the black vinegar, five-spice powder, sesame oil, white pepper, garlic, ginger, and salt in a small bowl.

2 Heat the sunflower oil in a large sauté pan over high heat. Sear the oyster mushrooms until crispy on all sides, about 5 minutes. Add the black vinegar marinade and bring to a boil, scraping up any crispy bits stuck to the pan. Simmer for 2 minutes, until the mixture starts to caramelize. Remove from the heat.

3 Heat the Pho Broth in a small saucepan over medium heat.

4 Spread the vegan mayo and sriracha on the baguette. Then stuff with the warm mushrooms and top with the basil, scallions, cilantro, and jalapeño slices (if using). Transfer the Pho Broth to serving bowls and serve alongside the sandwiches for easy dipping.

(recipe continues)

(recipe continued from previous page)

PHO BROTH

2 sticks cinnamon

8 pieces star anise (see other uses, below)

1 teaspoon white pepper

8 dried shiitake mushrooms

Four 1-inch pieces ginger (no need to peel, will be discarded)

1 tablespoon plus 1 teaspoon tamari

2 teaspoons five-spice powder

2 quarts Shiitake Dashi (page 130)

1 Combine all of the ingredients in a large stockpot with the dashi. Let soak for 20 minutes, then bring to a boil over high heat.

2 Immediately reduce the heat to low and simmer for 20 minutes.

3 Remove the broth from the heat and let it steep, covered, for 20 minutes.

4 Strain out solids.

MAKES 2 QUARTS

THREE OTHER USES FOR STAR ANISE

1. Add a few to your pickle brine for a licorice touch.

2. Simmer in tomato soup (1 piece per 2 quarts) as an alternative to fennel.

TRAVEL JOURNAL
IN SEARCH OF BRAZIL

Haunted by a vision of a place you have never been to. A place that captivates your imagination and calls you back as if you had once visited in another lifetime, a place you know well but you can't remember actually being there. Ireland does this easily, while for some it's Paris. For us, it was Brazil.

We touched down in the morning, after a long overnight flight. Restless and sleepless, we set off in search of sun, sand, and vegetarian *moqueca*, a fabled stew tingling with chiles, tomato, coconut, cilantro, and lime, that had captured our imagination.

Arriving at the Copacabana beach was one of the most magical travel moments. We were warned that you shouldn't go there after dark. Yet what we found was something much different: a clean, modern city anticipating the Olympics and ready to shine in the international spotlight. Off the beach strip, we wandered side streets up in the little neighborhood of Santa Teresa. Colorful old homes and little cafés tucked into the hills recalled Europe, but the palms and lush exotic foliage said otherwise.

We found a serene little pizza restaurant set in a garden and on the menu was our destiny: vegetarian moqueca! Our eyes wide and barely able to believe it, we dug our spoons deep down into the bowl to stir up the steaming aromatics and coat the rice next to it. It was delicious, spicy, herby, and creamy. An epic culinary postcard.

The night before our flight home, as the sun set, we sat at a beachside cafe sipping caipirinhas and eating papas fritas doused with malagueta hot sauce, taking in the spicy, salty, and sweet flavors of the surreal experience of just being there. We breathed in deep the thick sea air, our drinks heady with lime and cachaca, and we smiled, knowing that we were now part of our memories of Brazil.

BOWLS

Soondubu Jjigae 125

Chilled Spicy Sesame Noodles 127

Singapore Noodles 128

**Shiitake Dashi
with Charred Broccoli** 130

Spicy Chana Stew 131

V Street Ramen 132

Phat Udon 134

**Dan Dan Noodles
with Shiitake Mushrooms** 137

It's hard to put your finger on exactly what makes Korean food so special: the pungent pickles, the sweet-and-spicy fermented bean pastes, all the chiles. It's not a subtle cuisine. Soondubu jjigae, or soft tofu stew, is an excellent example. It's a cauldron of fiery, funky red broth that dares you keep going and finish the bowl. We've created an easy version that is guaranteed to make your kitchen smell awesome. Remember, if you use homemade kimchi, you can always customize this to your individual taste and pat yourself on the back for the extra effort! **SERVES 4 TO 6**

SOONDUBU JJIGAE

2 tablespoons sesame oil

½ cup diced onion

1 tablespoon minced garlic

4 cups finely chopped Napa cabbage

7 cups vegetable stock

2 cups kimchi

¼ cup tamari

2 tablespoons gochujang

2 teaspoons sugar

24 ounces soft tofu, rinsed and brought to room temperature, and cut to size of your choosing

½ cup chopped scallions (green parts only)

Black sesame seeds

1 Heat the sesame oil in a large stockpot over high heat until it ripples. Add the onion and garlic and sauté until brown, stirring occasionally, about 3 to 5 minutes.

2 Add the cabbage and continue to brown for an additional 3 to 5 minutes, stirring occasionally.

3 Add the stock, kimchi with its juice, tamari, gochujang, and sugar. Simmer for 15 minutes, stirring often.

4 Add 4 to 6 ounces of tofu to each serving bowl. Traditionally, a large piece is presented, but you can cut it into 1-inch cubes if desired.

5 Ladle the stew over the tofu. Garnish each bowl with the scallions and sesame seeds and serve.

THREE OTHER USES FOR BLACK VINEGAR

1. Add a couple splashes to a stir-fry for a nice sweet-and-sour flavor.

2. Add a little to your pickle brine to give another dimension of flavor.

3. Mix 1 tablespoon with 1 tablespoon agave syrup and 1 tablespoon soy sauce for a great teriyaki-like glaze you can use to finish vegetables.

Nothing beats a steaming bowl of noodles in the wintertime. There's something so soul warming about coming in from the cold and lifting that steaming soup spoon up to your shivering lips. But in the heat of the summer, a chilled noodle dish is the way to go, and soba noodles are the perfect canvas. This dish is easy to put together, and the dressed noodles taste just as good whether you enjoy them immediately or the day after, making this an ideal summertime meal. For those who love the flavor of buckwheat, look for soba noodles that have a high percentage of buckwheat. They are harder to work with but carry so much more flavor. Either way you'll love the snappy texture the noodles bring against this creamy, tangy sauce. **SERVES 4**

CHILLED SPICY SESAME NOODLES

SESAME SAUCE

¼ cup black vinegar (see tip, opposite)

1 teaspoon sugar

2 tablespoons sriracha

2 tablespoons tamari

1 teaspoon chile oil

2 teaspoons sesame oil

¼ cup chopped scallions (white parts only)

3 tablespoons tahini

12 ounces dry soba noodles

Chopped scallions (green parts only) and sesame seeds for garnish

1 Combine all of the sesame sauce ingredients in a medium bowl and whisk together until smooth. Any left over can be stored in the refrigerator for up to 5 days.

2 Prepare an ice water bath of 4 quarts water with 1 quart ice. Bring a large pot of water to a boil and cook the noodles according to package instructions. Once tender, drain the noodles and immediately plunge into the ice water bath to stop the cooking.

3 Drain the noodles from the ice water bath, transfer to a medium bowl, and toss gently with the sesame sauce until evenly coated. Garnish with the scallions and sesame seeds before serving.

Singapore: a bustling, multicultural melting pot of Malay, Indian, and Chinese. A contrast of ultramodern architecture against quaint old homes, shops, and temples. The food here is all over the place, and that's how we ate. Indian here, Chinese there, Japanese, Indonesian, and Malaysian. From fine dining to dumpling houses and street food hawker centers. But our search for actual Singapore noodles came up empty. Singapore noodles, a longtime fixture on V Street's menu, are actually a dish that exists all over the world. Just not in Singapore. But that's okay; these simple rice noodles touched with curry, white pepper, chile, and ginger embody all things great about the mix of food in Singapore. **SERVES 2 TO 4**

SINGAPORE NOODLES

14 ounces dried rice noodles

2 heads broccoli

1 tablespoon sesame oil

½ teaspoon salt

½ teaspoon pepper

Singapore Sauce (opposite)

Char Siu Tempeh (page 22)

Sambal oelek, fresh lime
     wedges, for serving

1 Cook the rice noodles according to package instructions.

2 Cut the broccoli heads in half. Blanch in salted, boiling water for about 3 minutes, then drain and cut into florets. Season the broccoli with sesame oil, salt, and pepper.

3 Chargrill the broccoli for 3 to 5 minutes or place under a broiler in the oven for 2 to 3 minutes.

4 Heat the Singapore Sauce and broccoli in a saucepan until a soft boil is reached.

5 Throw in the cooked rice noodles and boil for 10 seconds.

6 Remove from the heat.

7 Top with Char Siu Tempeh and serve with a side of sambal oelek and some fresh lime wedges.

SINGAPORE SAUCE

1½ tablespoons curry powder

2 tablespoons plus
  ¾ teaspoon tamari

1⅕ teaspoons rice wine
  vinegar

1½ tablespoons mirin

1½ tablespoons sesame oil

1½ teaspoons white pepper

1½ quarts Pho Broth
  (page 120)

½ tablespoon five-spice
  powder

1 teaspoon sugar

1½ tablespoons sambal oelek

1 Blend all the ingredients in a blender except for
the sambal.

2 Whisk in the sambal oelek by hand.

MAKES 1½ QUARTS

Dashi is the foundation of Japanese cuisine. Unfortunately for vegetarians it is made with powdered fish and seaweed, which gives it its powerful umami punch. We have created (and perfected over years) a version of dashi that doesn't sacrifice any umami whatsoever by using dried shiitakes and kombu seaweed. Like Japanese food itself, it is so very simple and clean; in fact, we often sip it like tea on cold Philly winter days.

It's great as is but feel free to add ginger, leeks, or celery to give it an extra dimension. To really go over the top, try adding grilled onions for a rich, smoky kick. **MAKES 2 QUARTS**

SHIITAKE DASHI WITH CHARRED BROCCOLI

1½ cups dried shiitake mushrooms

2 ounces kombu (about 2 to 3 sheets)

¼ cup tamari

2 heads charred broccoli (see page 128)

1 Combine all of the ingredients with 2 quarts water in a medium stockpot over high heat and bring to a boil.

2 Reduce the heat to low and simmer for 15 minutes.

3 Remove from the heat and let steep for 5 minutes.

4 Strain out the solids. Store in the refrigerator for up to 1 week.

We love beautiful Caribbean beaches as much as the next person, but an equally compelling reason to get on a plane in the depths of winter is the unbelievably addictive power of Caribbean food. Many people are surprised to find curry in the Caribbean, but it is indeed a staple down there, brought over by Indian indentured servants and mingled with that great culinary melting pot from the Americas, Africa, and Spain. This chana stew starts off classically enough but then takes a sunny turn south with a jerk sauce to enhance the aromatics in the curry. We serve this with socca chickpea crepes. **SERVES 4 TO 6**

SPICY CHANA STEW

2 tablespoons sunflower oil

1 tablespoon curry powder

2 teaspoons cumin

1 cup chopped onion

2 garlic cloves, minced

¼ cup chopped jalapeño pepper (substitute bell pepper for less intense heat)

2 cups chickpeas, drained and rinsed

1 cup chopped plum tomato

2 teaspoons sea salt

1 teaspoon freshly ground black pepper

1 teaspoon sriracha

1 tablespoon Jerk Sauce (page 206)

Cooked jasmine rice or Socca (page 104), for serving

1 Heat the sunflower oil, curry powder, and cumin in a medium sauté pan over high heat until the oil ripples. Sauté the onion, garlic, and jalapeño until the onion browns, 3 to 4 minutes.

2 Add the chickpeas, tomato, salt, and pepper, and cook for another 3 minutes.

3 Stir in the sriracha, jerk sauce, and ½ cup water, then simmer for another 5 minutes.

4 Serve over jasmine rice or stuffed inside chickpea crepes.

A good ramen bowl is a work of art. Much like pho helps define Vietnamese cuisine, ramen is an integral part of Japanese cooking with regional differences and personal preferences yielding a huge range of interpretations of this simple noodle and broth dish. Ours begins with our Shiitake Dashi, enriched with the condensed sweet-and-salty punch of canned corn juice, a strange but effective tip we picked up from a ramen shop we visited in D.C. This creates a wonderful mouthfeel in the broth—the perfect canvas for all your inventive creativity. **SERVES 4 TO 6**

V STREET RAMEN

4 cups Shiitake Dashi (page 130)

1 teaspoon tamari

2 teaspoons white miso paste

1 teaspoon sesame oil

1 teaspoon minced ginger

1 teaspoon minced garlic

½ teaspoon mirin

2 teaspoons canned corn juice, optional

24 ounces fresh ramen noodles (substitute 16 ounces dry noodles)

Vegetables: charred broccoli and grilled bok choy or grilled shiitake mushroom caps, pickled cucumber, shredded cabbage, and baked tofu (as shown)

Slivered nori and scallions (green parts only) for garnish

1 Combine all of the ingredients except the noodles, vegetables, and garnishes in a large saucepan over medium heat, bring to a boil, and boil for 10 minutes. Reduce the heat to low and keep warm.

2 Meanwhile, bring a large pot of water to a boil. Prepare the ramen noodles according to package directions. Drain.

3 Divide the ramen noodles among the serving bowls, then ladle in the broth. Arrange the additional vegetables on top of the noodles. Garnish with the nori and scallions.

There is something poetic about watching people eat noodles in Asia. There is a grace, a meditation, a beautiful and profound sense of movement as chopsticks dance through a steamy bowl in effortless motions that transcend eating and become more of a ballet between human and food. There is nothing like the warming vision of a steaming bowl of noodle soup landing in front of you. You admire, you stir, you taste and twirl. Our deep relationship to soup exists in every culture, and this one combines ingredients and inspirations from all over Asia into a super-satisfying dish that you will find easy to prepare. **SERVES 4 TO 6**

PHAT UDON

1 tablespoon plus 1 teaspoon sea salt

6 baby bok choy, cleaned and halved

1 tablespoon sesame oil

Freshly ground black pepper

½ cup diced turnips

Canola oil for frying

Two 8-ounce packages fresh thick udon noodles (substitute 16 ounces dry noodles)

1½ quarts Shiitake Dashi (page 130)

1 cup slivered marinated, baked tofu, such as five-spice (see tip, opposite)

1 cup sliced scallions (green parts only)

6 ounces snow pea shoots

1 Bring 4 quarts water and 1 tablespoon of the salt to a boil in a medium stockpot over high heat. Prepare an ice water bath of 4 quarts water with 1 quart ice.

2 Blanch the baby bok choy halves for 30 seconds. Transfer to the ice water bath to stop the cooking.

3 Drain the bok choy, coat with the sesame oil, and season with the remaining 1 teaspoon salt and the pepper.

4 Grill lightly on both sides on a hot grill or grill pan, about 2 minutes on each side (protect the delicate leaves as much as possible and try to get nice marks on the base). Cut into ½-inch pieces.

5 Line a sheet pan with paper towels. Heat 2 inches of canola oil in a medium skillet or sauté pan over high heat until the oil begins to ripple. Fry the turnips in oil for about 1 minute, until the edges are golden brown.

6 Remove the turnips from the oil with a strainer and spread them out in a single layer on the paper towel–lined sheet pan until cool.

7 Combine the noodles and dashi in a large stockpot. Bring to a boil and cook the noodles according to package instructions.

8 In a medium sauté pan or wok, heat more canola oil over medium-high heat until it ripples. Stir-fry the tofu strips for 2 to 3 minutes for color.

9 Evenly divide the soup and noodles among serving bowls. Top with the bok choy and tofu and garnish with fried turnips, scallions, and snow pea shoots.

We love five-spice-flavored tofu, but sesame-ginger and teriyaki-flavored will also work in this recipe.

One of the original street foods of the world, this amazing Szechuan dish was once served by vendors walking around with a stick across their shoulders. On one end hung a pot with some hot broth and on the other end was a pot with the noodles. It eventually evolved into one of the spicier Szechuan offerings, and then on its arrival to the States the spices were tamed to please more palates. We've kept our V Street version of this dish pretty spicy. If you can't hang, then by all means cut back on the sauce. We use fresh ramen noodles here, but any noodle you choose (even spaghetti!) will work just fine if cooked properly. **SERVES 6**

DAN DAN NOODLES WITH SHIITAKE MUSHROOMS

1 tablespoon black vinegar

¼ cup sesame oil

½ teaspoon white pepper

1 teaspoon minced garlic

1 teaspoon minced ginger

1 teaspoon five-spice powder

1 teaspoon sea salt

½ pound shiitake mushroom caps, sliced into ¼-inch-thin strips

Dan Dan Sauce (page 138)

24 ounces fresh ramen noodles (substitute 16 ounces dry noodles of choice)

½ cup chopped scallions (green parts only)

1 Preheat the oven to 450°F. Combine the black vinegar, sesame oil, white pepper, garlic, ginger, five-spice powder, and salt together in a medium bowl. Whisk until thoroughly combined.

2 Toss the mushrooms in the vinaigrette and place in a single layer on a sheet pan. Roast for 10 minutes or until crispy on the edges.

3 Warm the dan dan sauce in a small saucepan over low heat.

4 Bring a large pot of salted water to a boil. Cook the noodles according to package instructions. When tender, drain them immediately and add to the dan dan sauce, tossing gently to coat evenly.

5 Transfer the noodles to serving bowls and top with the shiitake caps and scallions.

(recipe continues)

(recipe continued from previous page)

DAN DAN SAUCE

¼ cup sriracha

¼ cup tahini

¼ cup tamari

1 tablespoon sesame oil

¼ teaspoon chile oil

½ teaspoon Szechuan peppercorns

1 small pickled chile with oil, optional

¼ teaspoon sugar

¾ cup vegetable stock

Combine all of the ingredients in a blender and blend until smooth. Store in an airtight container in the refrigerator for up to 1 week. Always stir before using.

MAKES 2 CUPS

TRAVEL JOURNAL
TOKYO NOODLE BARS

We touched down in Asia for the first time in 2008. We were very excited to travel so far, and had little idea what to expect in Tokyo. Between language barriers and time zone changes, jet lag and foreign currency exchanges, the last thing we needed was to worry about how to find vegetarian food. But any worry soon faded as we eased into what was undoubtedly the most important culinary adventure of our life. We learned about the vegetarian heyday of the Edo period in Japan, and, barring a little omnipresent dashi, we soon discovered that Japanese food culture—much like France's—is an incredibly reverent one that holds the pristine qualities of purity of ingredients and the skillfulness and dedication of its cooks in extremely high regard.

One morning when we ventured into downtown Tokyo and found ourselves politely stumbling through the Akihabara Electric Town, we entered a noodle shop and had our first taste of proper Japanese noodles. Instead of the sweet, sticky limp mess you might find Stateside, we were served the most perfect soba with just the right amount of *koshi* (the textural tug-of-war you play when your noodles are cooked perfectly) and with a touch of tamari, scallions, and sesame seeds for accents. We slurped happily along with our neighbors while proud women of a certain age buzzed around the room delivering the largest glass mugs of beer we'd ever seen outside of Germany. Naturally, we found ourselves stopping into every noodle shop we could find after that, sampling the differences among ramen, soba, and udon, noticing the different textures and temperatures and flavors. It took some trial and error back at home, but now, these many years later, we like to think we do right by those Japanese noodle chefs—some of the most inspiring chefs we'll probably ever have the pleasure of meeting.

SWEETS

Churro Ice Cream Sandwich 142

Togarashi Caramel Corn 144

Halo Halo with Sweet Potato Ice Cream 145

Halva Ice Cream with Sour Cherries 148

Lemongrass Ice Cream with Cardamom Puffed Rice Treats 150

Blackberry Ais Kacang with Sweet Corn Ice Cream 153

Sesame Rice Balls 157

Sweet Potato Arancini 159

Pelamushi 163

Coconut Torrejas with Guava Butter 164

Chocolate–Peanut Butter Waffles with Curry-Banana Ice Cream 166

Chocolate-Covered Cherry Alfajores 170

We move a lot of soft serve at V Street. Sometimes when we're anxious to get on to a new flavor, we end with a little left over. On one particularly creative evening, we decided to freeze the leftovers into little rounds. The next morning, we prepped some tasty churro pastry dough, rolled it into little disks, and fried them off so we could roll them in cinnamon sugar and stack them around the ice cream pucks. And so was born the ultimate ice cream sandwich. **SERVES 6**

CHURRO ICE CREAM SANDWICH

1 teaspoon sea salt

2 teaspoons brown sugar

1 tablespoon baking powder

1 tablespoon olive oil

2 cups flour plus more for dusting

½ cup granulated sugar

1 tablespoon cinnamon

Canola oil for frying

1 pint of your favorite vegan ice cream

1 Combine 2 cups water, the salt, brown sugar, baking powder, and olive oil in a medium saucepan and bring to a boil over medium heat. Whisk in the flour, stirring constantly just until fully combined, about 30 seconds.

2 Transfer the dough to a plate, cover with plastic wrap, and let cool to room temperature, about 20 minutes.

3 Line a sheet pan with parchment paper. On a floured work surface, roll the dough out into a ½-inch sheet and use a cookie cutter to stamp out twelve 2-inch circles. Arrange the churros on the baking pan. Cover the pan tightly in plastic wrap and freeze until ready to fry, up to 1 week.

4 Line a plate with paper towels. Combine the granulated sugar and cinnamon in a small bowl and set aside. Preheat a fryer to 375°F or heat 2 inches of the oil in a large skillet or saucepan over high heat until the oil begins to ripple. Fry the churros, 2 to 4 at a time, for 4 minutes or until golden brown.

5 Remove the churros from the heat and drain on the paper towel–lined plate for 1 minute to remove any excess oil. Lightly roll the churros in the cinnamon sugar. Place on a rack to cool for at least 5 minutes.

6 Place a scoop of your favorite ice cream on a cooled churro and press a second churro on top to make a sandwich. Serve immediately.

We like to keep a little somethin'-somethin' around for an after-dinner snack. It's intended for our guests, but it's nice to have something sweet for us to snack on too! This caramel corn hits the spot—it's a touch salty, not too sweet, with a perfect crunch and just a little tingle of heat. **SERVES 4 TO 6**

TOGARASHI CARAMEL CORN

2 teaspoons sesame oil

½ cup popcorn kernels

1 cup granulated sugar

1 tablespoon vegan butter

1 tablespoon miso

1 teaspoon black vinegar

1 teaspoon tamari

½ teaspoon baking soda

1 teaspoon Togarashi (page 201)

1 Heat the sesame oil in a large saucepan over medium heat. Add the popcorn kernels and cover with a lid. Keep the pan moving a bit until the popping slows, about 2½ minutes. Remove the pan from the heat and transfer the popcorn to a large metal or glass bowl.

2 Combine the sugar, butter, and ¼ cup water in a medium saucepan and heat over high heat for about 5 minutes, until the sugar caramelizes and reaches 300°F. If you don't have a candy thermometer, watch for the bubbles to become fat and slow, and the sugar will pull a bit from the sides of the pan. You can also use the hard crack test by dripping a tiny bit of sugar from a spoon into a glass of water and watch the sugar break into little threads. It will yield a nice, crispy crunch on your caramel corn. Remove the caramel from the heat and carefully whisk in the miso, black vinegar, and tamari, then the baking soda.

3 Very carefully, pour the caramel over the popcorn, then sprinkle with the togarashi and carefully toss the popcorn to coat evenly. Cool fully before storing in an airtight container at room temperature for up to 5 days—if it lasts that long.

If you sit down for a meal at V Street, chances are you'll have a few fiery small plates cross your table. To cool things down, we always have at least one refreshing ice cream–type dessert available, and one of our favorites hails from the Philippines. Halo halo (the Tagalog word for "mixed up") is a winning combination of ice cream and shaved ice with sweetened condensed milk, gummies, and fruits. There's no one defining recipe, so you can let your imagination run wild. We use a granita in place of shaved ice and coconut whipped cream to add extra richness. **SERVES 4 TO 6**

HALO HALO WITH SWEET POTATO ICE CREAM

½ cup chopped pineapple

½ cup black-eyed peas

½ cup pomegranate seeds

1 teaspoon agave syrup

1 teaspoon lime juice

2 cups Sweet Potato Ice Cream (page 147)

1½ cups Orange Granita (below)

1 cup Coconut Whipped Cream (page 146)

¼ cup toasted coconut flakes

1 Combine the pineapple, peas, pomegranate seeds, agave syrup, and lime juice in a small bowl and toss gently to evenly coat.

2 Transfer to an airtight container and store in the refrigerator for up to 3 days.

3 Alternate layers of ice cream, granita, whipped cream, toasted coconut flakes, and the fruit salad in clear parfait glasses. Top with additional whipped cream as desired and garnish with the remaining toasted coconut flakes.

ORANGE GRANITA

1 cup sugar

1 cup orange juice

2 tablespoons lemon juice

1 teaspoon vanilla extract

1 teaspoon orange zest

1 Bring the sugar and 1 cup water to a boil in a medium saucepan over medium-high heat. Reduce

(recipe continues)

(recipe continued from previous page)

the heat to medium and simmer for about 5 minutes, until the mixture forms a thick syrup.

2 Remove from the heat and allow to cool fully before transferring to a bowl with the remaining ingredients. Transfer to an airtight container and place in the freezer, stirring three times during the first 30 minutes to get a sweet icy mixture (rather than a layer of oozy sugar on the bottom and ice crystals on the top). This will store in the freezer for up to 2 weeks.

MAKES ABOUT 2 CUPS

COCONUT WHIPPED CREAM

One 13-ounce can coconut milk
2 tablespoons confectioners' sugar

Place the coconut milk and confectioners' sugar in a medium bowl and whisk vigorously by hand for 5 minutes or in a stand mixer on high speed with the whisk attachment for 3 minutes (see tip). Transfer to an airtight container and store in the refrigerator for up to 2 days.

MAKES ABOUT 2 CUPSS

———

At the restaurant, we combine the ingredients in a whipped cream canister for airy, fluffy whipped cream. If you're an ice cream aficionado, this will take your sundaes to the next level.

SWEET POTATO ICE CREAM

1½ cups chopped purple sweet
    potato (substitute orange
    sweet potato)

1 teaspoon sunflower oil

¾ cup sugar

2 cups coconut milk

1 teaspoon vanilla extract

1 tablespoon lime juice

1 Begin by preheating the oven to 400°F. Toss the sweet potatoes with the sunflower oil, transfer to a sheet pan, and roast for about 10 minutes, or just until tender.

2 Bring the sugar and 1 cup water to a boil in a medium saucepan over medium-high heat. Reduce the heat to medium and cook for 3 minutes, until the mixture forms a thick syrup.

3 Add the roasted potatoes and coconut milk to the syrup and simmer for an additional 5 minutes.

4 Remove from the heat, transfer to a blender, add the vanilla extract, and blend until smooth.

5 Transfer the contents to a bowl and refrigerate for 1 hour. Stir in the lime juice. Freeze the mixture in an ice cream maker according to the manufacturer's instructions. Store in an airtight container in the freezer for up to 1 week.

MAKES 1½ QUARTS

We knew soft serve would be an integral part of our dessert menu at V Street. We did not, however, realize that a soft-serve machine would cost more than some cars or that it requires about a day's worth of labor to keep it tuned up each week! But the ice creams themselves are so good, so decadent, so downright unfair, we could never turn back. Halva was the first flavor we introduced on our menu. Its creaminess is complemented by the tart flavor burst in the sour cherries. **SERVES 4 TO 6**

HALVA ICE CREAM WITH SOUR CHERRIES

1 cup sugar

2 cups soy milk

1 cup tahini

1 teaspoon vanilla extract

2 teaspoons lemon juice

½ teaspoon salt

Sour Cherries (opposite)

1 Bring the sugar and 1 cup water to a boil in a medium saucepan over medium-high heat. Reduce the heat to medium and cook for 5 minutes, until the mixture forms a thick syrup.

2 Remove from the heat and stir in the soy milk. Let the mixture cool fully before transferring it to a blender. Add the remaining ingredients except sour cherries and blend until smooth. Transfer the contents to a bowl and refrigerate for about 1 hour, or until chilled.

3 Freeze the mixture in an ice cream maker according to the manufacturer's instructions. Store in an airtight container in the freezer for up to 1 week.

4 Serve topped with sour cherries.

SOUR CHERRIES

¼ cup sugar

2 cups fresh or frozen pitted sour cherries (substitute any cherry; if using frozen, thaw and drain before use)

½ teaspoon vanilla extract

1 tablespoon cornstarch

1 Bring the sugar and ½ cup water to a boil in a medium saucepan over medium-high heat. Reduce the heat to medium, then add the cherries and vanilla extract. Cook until the cherries soften, about 4 minutes.

2 Combine the cornstarch and 2 tablespoons water to create a slurry. Add to the cherries and bring just to a boil, then remove from the heat.

3 Once fully cool, transfer to an airtight container and store in the refrigerator for up to 5 days.

One of our most successful ice creams combines lemongrass with candied kumquats for a flavor that is reminiscent of that popular rainbow cereal that looks like fruit rings—you know the one, right? This ice cream is sweet and bright, floral with just a touch of bitter marmalade from the kumquat skins. This is a great wintertime dessert when kumquats are in season, and the Cardamom Puffed Rice Treats make for a delightful, crunchy garnish. **SERVES 4 TO 6**

LEMONGRASS ICE CREAM WITH CARDAMOM PUFFED RICE TREATS

1 cup sugar

½ cup lemongrass pulp
(see tip, below)

2 cups coconut milk

1 teaspoon vanilla extract

2 tablespoons lime juice

1 cup Cardamom Puffed Rice
Treats (opposite)

½ cup Kumquat Marmalade
(opposite)

1 Bring the sugar and 1 cup water to a boil in a medium saucepan over medium-high heat. Reduce the heat to medium and cook until a thick syrup forms, about 5 minutes. Add the lemongrass pulp and simmer for an additional 5 minutes.

2 Remove from the heat then stir in the coconut milk. Allow to cool fully, transfer to a blender, and add the vanilla and lime juice. Blend until smooth, then strain into a bowl. Chill in the refrigerator about 1 hour.

3 Freeze the mixture in an ice cream maker according to the manufacturer's instructions. Store in an airtight container in the freezer for up to 1 week. Serve topped with Cardamom Puffed Rice Treats and Kumquat Marmalade.

———

If you have beautiful, fresh lemongrass, you can pound the bases with the back of a knife and peel the outer layers to collect the pulp. But don't be afraid to use frozen lemongrass too. It's much easier and more consistent, and you're just going to freeze it again anyway!

KUMQUAT MARMALADE

½ cup sugar

1 cup kumquats, stems removed, sliced into ¼-inch-thick rings

½ vanilla bean, split

1 star anise

1 Bring the sugar and 1 cup water to a boil in a medium saucepan over medium-high heat. Reduce the heat to medium then add the kumquats, vanilla bean, and star anise. Cover and cook for about 10 minutes, or until the kumquats soften.

2 Remove from the heat and cool fully. Transfer to an airtight container and store in the refrigerator for up to 1 week.

CARDAMOM PUFFED RICE TREATS

2 tablespoons agave syrup

1 teaspoon cardamom

¼ teaspoon cinnamon

⅛ teaspoon sea salt

½ cup puffed rice cereal

1 Preheat the oven to 400°F.

2 Whisk together the agave syrup, spices, and salt in a medium bowl. Add the puffed rice cereal, toss gently to evenly coat, and transfer to a parchment-lined baking sheet. Toast until golden brown, about 5 minutes. Let cool fully before transferring to an airtight container. Store at room temperature for up to 5 days.

Building on our Southeast Asian ice-dessert repertoire, Malaysia's ais kacang is another fun way to beat the heat (both temperature and spice level)! Ais kacang translates into "ice beans," and here we fold a few adzuki beans into our parfait along with a rich, creamy corn custard ice cream and tangy blackberry granita in place of the traditional shaved ice. The basil seeds on top are a fun, colorful garnish, making the dish all that much more visually intriguing. **SERVES 4 TO 6**

BLACKBERRY AIS KACANG WITH SWEET CORN ICE CREAM

½ cup adzuki beans

½ cup grilled corn kernels

1 teaspoon plus 2 tablespoons agave syrup

1 teaspoon lime juice

¼ cup basil seeds (see tip, page 154) plus more for garnish

¼ cup basil leaves

1 teaspoon lemon juice

2 cups Sweet Corn Ice Cream (page 155)

1½ cups Blackberry Granita (page 154)

1 cup Coconut Whipped Cream (page 146)

1 Combine the adzuki beans, grilled corn kernels, 1 teaspoon of the agave syrup, and lime juice in a small bowl, and toss gently to evenly coat. Transfer to an airtight container and store in the refrigerator for up to 3 days.

2 In a separate bowl, combine the basil seeds with ½ cup water. Soak for several minutes, until the seeds fully absorb the water.

3 Meanwhile, combine ½ cup water with the remaining 2 tablespoons agave syrup and basil leaves in a blender and blend until smooth.

4 Strain the contents of the blender into the bowl with the basil seeds. Add the lemon juice and stir to evenly combine before transferring to an airtight container. Store in the refrigerator for up to 5 days.

5 Alternate layers of ice cream, granita, adzuki bean mixture, and whipped cream in clear parfait glasses. Top with additional whipped cream as desired and garnish with basil seeds before serving.

(recipe continues)

(recipe continued from previous page)

THREE OTHER USES FOR BASIL SEEDS

1. Mix with equal parts chia seeds for the ultimate chia pudding.

2. Fold into your favorite cookie recipe (1 teaspoon seeds per cup of flour) in place of poppy seeds or sesame seeds just before baking.

3. Mix with equal parts sesame seeds to garnish maki rolls.

BLACKBERRY GRANITA

½ cup sugar

2 cups fresh or frozen blackberries (if using frozen, thaw and drain)

¼ cup orange juice

1 teaspoon vanilla extract

1 teaspoon lemon zest

1 teaspoon lemon juice

1 Bring the sugar and 1 cup water to a boil in a medium saucepan over medium-high heat. Reduce the heat to medium and simmer for about 2 minutes, until the mixture forms a thick syrup. Add the blackberries just before removing from the heat.

2 Allow the mixture to cool fully before transferring it to a blender. Add the orange juice, vanilla, lemon zest, and lemon juice, and blend until smooth. Strain to remove the blackberry seeds, then transfer the mixture to an airtight container and place in the freezer, stirring occasionally for the first 30 minutes. Store in the freezer for up to 2 weeks.

MAKES 2 CUPS

SWEET CORN ICE CREAM

3/4 cup sugar

2 cups fresh or frozen corn kernels (if using frozen, thaw and drain)

1 cup coconut milk

1 teaspoon vanilla extract

2 tablespoons lime juice

1 Bring the sugar and 1 cup water to a boil in a medium saucepan over medium-high heat. Reduce the heat to medium and simmer for about 3 minutes, or until the mixture forms a thick syrup.

2 Add the corn kernels and coconut milk and simmer for about 5 minutes, until the corn is cooked.

3 Remove from the heat, transfer to a blender, add the vanilla extract, and blend until smooth.

4 Strain into a bowl and place in the refrigerator for 1/2 hour, or until fully chilled. Stir in the lime juice. Freeze the mixture in an ice cream maker according to the manufacturer's instructions. Store in an airtight container in the freezer for up to 1 week.

MAKES 1½ QUARTS

Most Americans who come home from an extended stay in Asia are craving any bready foods they can get their hands on: pizza, burgers—you get the picture. The same can be said about desserts. Many Southeast Asian countries work a lot with ices and custards, then up in Japan, China, and Korea you'll see a focus on lightly sweet desserts, jellies, and lots of rice flour dumplings and buns. Beans play a huge role too. At V Street, we like to highlight some of the best of these sweet notes, and these crispy, lightly salty snacks are a great not-too-sweet after-dinner treat. **SERVES 6 TO 8**

SESAME RICE BALLS

¾ cup brown sugar

1 teaspoon tamari

3 cups glutinous rice flour

¼ cup rice flour plus a little extra for dusting

½ cup sesame seeds (or as needed)

1 cup red bean paste (see tip, page 158)

Canola oil for frying

1 Bring 1 cup water to a rolling boil in a small saucepan over medium heat. Add the brown sugar and tamari, let the sugar dissolve, then remove from the heat.

2 Combine the rice flours in a medium bowl and make a well in the center. Pour the water mixture in the well and stir with a spoon to create a sticky dough. Set aside to cool for 15 minutes.

3 Meanwhile, coat a large dinner plate with the sesame seeds.

4 Transfer the dough to a lightly floured work surface and divide into golf ball–size pieces, about 16 total. Roll each piece into a ball.

5 Indent the balls with your thumb and place 1 tablespoon of the bean paste in the center, pinch the hole closed and smooth over, then roll in the sesame seeds to coat evenly.

(recipe continues)

(recipe continued from previous page)

6 Line a plate with paper towels. Preheat a fryer to 350°F or heat 2 inches of canola oil in a large saucepan over high heat just until the oil ripples on the surface.

7 Fry 4 to 6 balls at a time until golden brown, about 3 minutes. Transfer to the paper towel–lined plate to absorb any excess oil then serve immediately. Store any leftover rice balls in an airtight container in the refrigerator for up to 2 days, bringing to room temperature before serving again.

———

Make your own red bean paste by mashing together 1 cup cooked red beans with 1 tablespoon agave syrup.

Sicily has got to be one of the very best spots for street food if for no other reason than the glorious arancini! Of course, most people think of savory arancini, but we developed this recipe with our dessert menu in mind. We put an Asian spin on the recipe by using jasmine rice and coconut milk for the rice pudding, and stuffed the arancini with a tangy sweet potato filling. These are delicious solo but are even tastier when served with a little ponzu-maple dipping sauce (see tip, page 161). **SERVES 4**

SWEET POTATO ARANCINI

RICE PUDDING
1 teaspoon coconut oil

1 cinnamon stick

1 star anise

Two 16-ounce cans coconut milk

1 cup jasmine rice, rinsed

Seeds from ½ vanilla bean

¼ cup sugar

¼ cup cornstarch

SWEET POTATO FILLING
2 cups peeled and chopped
   sweet potato

1 teaspoon sesame oil

1 teaspoon five-spice powder

¼ cup light brown sugar

2 tablespoons black vinegar

1 teaspoon sriracha

Pinch of sea salt

Canola oil for frying

Rice flour for dusting

1 Combine the coconut oil, cinnamon stick, and star anise in a large pot over low heat and heat for 1 minute.

2 Add the coconut milk, 2 cups water, rice, and vanilla seeds to the pot. Cook, stirring frequently, for about 15 minutes, just until the rice turns tender.

3 Add the sugar and cook for another 5 minutes, until the sugar is dissolved and the rice pudding thickens.

4 Remove the mixture from the heat and allow to cool fully then fold in the cornstarch. If making ahead, transfer to an airtight container and store in the refrigerator for up to 12 days.

5 Preheat the oven to 400°F. Toss the sweet potatoes with the sesame oil and five-spice powder in a medium bowl. Transfer to a sheet pan and bake for 15 minutes or until tender and starting to caramelize.

6 Return the sweet potatoes to the bowl, add the brown sugar, black vinegar, sriracha, and salt, then mash with a fork just until fluffy and well combined.

(recipe continues)

(recipe continued from previous page)

7 Line a plate with paper towels. Preheat a fryer to 375°F or heat 2 inches of canola oil in a saucepan over high heat until the oil starts to ripple.

8 Meanwhile, scoop the rice pudding into 12 large golf ball–size chunks and form each into a ball. Use your fingers to hollow out the centers of the balls and stuff with about 1$\frac{1}{2}$ tablespoons of sweet potato filling. Close the rice pudding balls neatly and roll lightly in the rice flour.

9 Fry the arancini, about 4 at a time, for 3 to 4 minutes, or until golden brown. Transfer to the paper towel–lined plate to absorb any excess oil then serve immediately.

———

Combine 1 tablespoon ponzu with $\frac{1}{4}$ cup maple syrup for a sweet-and-salty dipping sauce.

Georgian food is all the rage! Well, maybe that's true only in New York City, but it's wonderful news for vegetarians, as Georgian food is traditionally very friendly for plant-based diners thanks to strict orthodox lenten observance. While the traditional Georgian supra, the extravagant feast of about a bazillion different colorful dishes, may be a nightmare for the host preparing it, it's a dream come true for diners—an unimaginable assortment of breads, salads, stews, and dumplings. Dessert is fun too, showcasing the region's prized grapes in a fruity pudding called pelamushi. **SERVES 4 TO 6**

PELAMUSHI

½ cup walnut pieces

1 tablespoon vegan butter

2 tablespoons granulated sugar

1 teaspoon sea salt

3 cups red grape juice

1 cup red wine

¼ cup brown sugar

1 teaspoon vanilla extract

5 tablespoons cornstarch

1 tablespoon lemon juice

1 Toast the walnut pieces in a large sauté pan over medium heat until golden brown, about 2 minutes. Remove from the heat and add the vegan butter, sugar, and ½ teaspoon of the salt, stirring to ensure the walnut pieces are evenly coated. Cool fully before transferring to an airtight container and storing at room temperature for up to 1 week.

2 Combine the grape juice and red wine in a large saucepan over high heat and bring to a boil. Reduce the heat to medium and simmer for about 10 minutes until the liquid has reduced by half.

3 Transfer the mixture and the remaining ingredients to a blender, then blend carefully until smooth. Return the mixture to the saucepan, place over high heat, bring to a boil, and boil for 1 minute. Strain carefully into a serving dish or divide evenly among individual ramekins. Cool at room temperature for 20 minutes before transferring to the refrigerator to chill for 2 hours. Serve garnished with the candied walnuts.

All over the world, people find wonderful things to do with stale bread, whether it's panzanella salad in Italy or a good old-fashioned bread pudding whipped up for dessert. Many of these ideas are centered on breakfast food, and torrejas are the Latin world's answer to French toast. **SERVES 4**

COCONUT TORREJAS WITH GUAVA BUTTER

2 cups coconut milk

½ cup flour

2 teaspoons baking powder

½ teaspoon cinnamon

¼ teaspoon cloves

¼ teaspoon allspice

1½ teaspoons vanilla extract

½ cup unsweetened coconut flakes

¼ pound (1 stick) vegan butter, softened

¼ cup guava paste (see tip, opposite)

¾ teaspoon sea salt

1 teaspoon sugar

¼ teaspoon lime zest

1 teaspoon lime juice

½ cup maple syrup

2 teaspoons instant coffee grounds

1 teaspoon sherry vinegar

2 tablespoons sunflower oil

8 slices stale bread

1 Whisk together the coconut milk, flour, baking powder, cinnamon, cloves, allspice, 1 teaspoon of the vanilla extract, and the coconut flakes in a medium bowl.

2 Using a hand mixer or food processor, cream together the butter, guava paste, ½ teaspoon of the salt, sugar, lime zest, and lime juice. If making ahead, transfer the guava butter to an airtight container and keep refrigerated for up to 1 week.

3 Whisk together the maple syrup, instant coffee, sherry vinegar, remaining ¼ teaspoon salt, and remaining ½ teaspoon vanilla extract in a small bowl. If making ahead, transfer to an airtight container and keep refrigerated for up to 1 week.

4 Preheat the oven to warm, then heat ½ tablespoon of the sunflower oil in a large sauté pan over high heat. Dredge 2 slices of the stale bread in the batter and cook on one side until golden brown, about 2 minutes. Flip and cook on the other side until equally golden brown and crispy, about 2 more minutes. Transfer to a sheet pan and keep warm in the oven while repeating the process with the remaining oil and slices of bread.

5 Arrange the torrejas on serving dishes, spread with the guava butter, drizzle with the coffee-maple syrup, and serve.

THREE OTHER USES FOR GUAVA PASTE

1. Add ⅛ cup to 1 cup Huli Huli barbecue sauce (page 99) for something extra sweet and tangy.

2. Add to a vanilla ice cream base (½ cup per quart) with some fresh lime juice to make a creamy guava ice cream.

3. Blend ¼ cup paste with 1 tablespoon lemon juice and 1 tablespoone fresh chopped basil to create a syrup. Pour 2 ounces of the syrup over ice and top with 10 ounces of seltzer for a refreshing soda.

Waffles are serious street food in many parts of Europe, taking different shapes and forms from Scandinavia and south through Belgium and into France. You'll also find a wide range of interpretations throughout Asia, one of our favorites being a peanut butter waffle we sampled in Macau, a little island off mainland China. These crispy, toasty waffles are great for brunch, but we like to doll them up with bitter chocolate ganache, Curry-Banana Ice Cream, and Sriracha Peanuts for a decadent dessert. **SERVES 4 TO 6**

CHOCOLATE–PEANUT BUTTER WAFFLES WITH CURRY-BANANA ICE CREAM

1 cup flour

2 teaspoons baking powder

¼ teaspoon sea salt

2 teaspoons egg replacer powder

1 tablespoon brown sugar

1 cup soy milk

¼ cup plus 1 teaspoon
    sunflower oil

¼ cup peanut butter (see tip,
    page 169)

1 tablespoon sesame oil

½ teaspoon vanilla extract

1 cup Curry-Banana Ice Cream
    (page 169)

¼ cup Sriracha Peanuts
    (page 48)

CHOCOLATE GANACHE

1 cup bittersweet chocolate chips

¼ cup coconut milk
    (substitute soy milk)

1 teaspoon instant coffee
    grounds

⅛ teaspoon salt

1 Sift together the flour, baking powder, salt, and egg replacer in a large bowl.

2 In a separate bowl, whisk together the brown sugar, soy milk, ¼ cup of the sunflower oil, peanut butter, sesame oil, and vanilla extract. Add to the dry ingredients and whisk together until smooth.

3 Heat a waffle iron on high then lightly brush it with the remaining 1 teaspoon sunflower oil. (Alternatively, you could put a ring mold on a griddle or skillet and fill it to create a taller pancake.) Fill the iron with batter and cook until golden brown and crispy, about 4 minutes. Repeat with the remaining batter. (The batter will stay fresh stored airtight in the refrigerator for up to 24 hours.)

4 To make the chocolate ganache, melt the chocolate chips and coconut milk in a double boiler over low heat. Add the instant coffee and salt, whisking together to combine, then remove from the heat, cool fully, and transfer to an airtight container. Store in the refrigerator for up to 1 week.

(recipe continues)

(recipe continued from previous page)

5 Spread the waffles with the chocolate ganache and top with a scoop of Curry-Banana Ice Cream and a sprinkling of Sriracha Peanuts just before serving.

———

Omit both the peanut butter and sesame oil for a lighter, crispier waffle.

CURRY-BANANA ICE CREAM

1 cup sugar

2 cups sliced bananas

1 teaspoon curry powder

½ teaspoon turmeric

1 cup soy milk

1 cup coconut milk

1 teaspoon vanilla extract

2 teaspoons lime juice

½ teaspoon sea salt

1 Bring the sugar and 1 cup water to a boil in a medium saucepan over medium-high heat. Reduce the heat to medium and simmer for about 5 minutes, until the mixture forms a thick syrup. Add the bananas, curry powder, and turmeric, cover, and simmer covered on low for about 4 minutes, just until the bananas soften.

2 Remove from the heat and stir in the soy milk and coconut milk. Let the mixture cool fully before transferring to a blender. Blend with the remaining ingredients until smooth. Transfer to a bowl and refrigerate for about 1 hour, or until chilled.

3 Freeze the mixture in an ice cream maker according to the manufacturer's instructions. Store in an airtight container in the freezer for up to 1 week.

MAKES 1½ QUARTS

Home to the tango, Che Guevara, and most of Iguazu Falls, Argentina is a powerful force in South America. It is many things, but a good culinary destination for vegetarians it is not. At best, vegetarians will walk away with a spinach empanada, some grilled provoleta, and ice cream for dessert; vegans will do best sipping mate and Malbec. Argentina is also home to the alfajor, little sandwich cookies often filled with decadent dulce de leche and dipped in chocolate. Honoring the vibrant Jewish community in Argentina, we've pulled a little Middle Eastern flavor into this recipe with sesame and sumac to create a tasty dessert or teatime snack. **SERVES 8**

CHOCOLATE-COVERED CHERRY ALFAJORES

COOKIES

2 cups flour plus more for dusting

2 cups cornstarch

1 teaspoon baking powder

½ teaspoon sea salt

2 tablespoons egg replacer powder

1 cup confectioners' sugar

½ pound (2 sticks) vegan butter, softened

Zest and juice of 1 lemon

¼ cup arak (substitute other licorice-flavored liqueur)

1 Sift together the flour, cornstarch, baking powder, and salt in a medium bowl.

2 Beat together the egg replacer powder and ½ cup warm water in a small bowl using a hand mixer until the mixture becomes thick and foamy, about 3 minutes.

3 Beat together the sugar and butter in a separate medium bowl until creamy, about 3 minutes.

4 Fold the egg replacer mixture into the creamed butter along with the lemon zest, lemon juice, and arak.

5 Add the dry ingredients to the bowl and cut in until a soft dough ball forms. Divide the dough in half, wrap each ball in plastic wrap, and chill for at least 1 hour.

6 Preheat the oven to 350°F. Line a sheet pan with parchment paper. On a floured work surface, roll each dough ball very thin, no more than ⅛ inch

HALVA BUTTERCREAM

4 tablespoons (½ stick) vegan
butter, softened

2 tablespoons vegan shortening,
softened

1 cup confectioners' sugar

2 tablespoons tahini

Pinch of salt

½ teaspoon vanilla extract

CHERRY FILLING

¼ cup sugar

1 cup frozen cherries, thawed,
juices reserved

½ tablespoon cornstarch

Pinch of sumac

3 cups bittersweet chocolate
chips

thick, then use a cookie cutter to stamp out eight 3-inch circles from each dough ball. Arrange the cookies on the prepared sheet pan ½ inch apart. Bake for 10 minutes, or until just starting to brown. Allow to cool fully before removing them from the baking sheet. If making ahead, store in an airtight container at room temperature for up to 3 days.

7 To make the halva buttercream, beat together the butter and shortening using a mixer. Add the confectioners' sugar and tahini and continue beating until smooth and fluffy, about 3 minutes. Add the salt and vanilla extract and beat for 1 more minute. If making ahead, transfer to an airtight container and store in the refrigerator for up to 1 week.

8 To make the cherry filling, bring the sugar and reserved cherry juice to a boil in a medium saucepan over high heat. Cook for 3 minutes, or until the mixture is reduced by half. Add the cherries, and bring the mixture back to a boil. Remove 2 tablespoons of hot juice, and mix it with the cornstarch and sumac to create a slurry. Add the slurry back to the cherries and bring to a boil, about 1 minute. Remove from heat and let cool fully.

(recipe continues)

(recipe continued from previous page)

9 To assemble the cookies, place half the cookies on a work surface and pipe circles of buttercream just inside the edge. Place a spoonful of cherry filling in the center of that circle, then place another cookie on top to create a sandwich. Cover with plastic wrap and refrigerate for 20 minutes.

10 Meanwhile, melt 2 cups of the chocolate chips in a double boiler or microwave just until melted, 30 seconds. Remove from the heat and stir in the remaining 1 cup chocolate chips.

11 Remove the cookies from the refrigerator and place them on a cooling rack with a sheet pan underneath. Line another sheet pan with parchment paper. Pour the chocolate over the cookies, being sure to coat each one evenly. Transfer to the parchment-lined sheet pan and place in the refrigerator for at least 15 minutes to set the chocolate. Store the cookies in an airtight container in the refrigerator for up to 3 days until ready to serve.

TRAVEL JOURNAL
ROMAN PASTRY SHOPS

When you think of Italy, you think of pizza. Pasta. Maybe Chianti, or perhaps gelato. All these things are, of course, superior in Italy. But one thing that doesn't get much attention is the pastries. France gets the most love, Spain and Portugal get some notice, and even Austria is known for its sophisticated sweet tooth. But Italy has some of the most delicious pastries. Italians aren't afraid to fry their desserts or douse things in powdered sugar and colorful candied fruits.

So what if they're all named after people or holy days in the Catholic Church—Roman pastry shops are chock-full of delightful sweet treats. Beyond tiramisu and cannoli, there are *cornetti*, *bruttiboni*, *torrone*, *torta caprese*, and *maritozzi con la panna*.

Short of certain flavors at the delightfully colorful gelatto shops scattered across the city, most if not all of these are going to be nightmares for vegans, but it's such an inspiring scene—one that lends itself well to a street food culture of grabbing a little something at the pastry shop and settling into a sunny bench in the Villa Borghese for a romantic little picnic of some of the most joyful sweets you could imagine.

One of our favorite "dolce vita" inspirations is our cannoli soft serve: pistachio ice cream with chocolate Magic Shell, candied orange rind, and little chunks of fried cannoli shell. It's a great textural celebration of what we love most in Italy.

COCKTAILS

Tiger's Purr 176

Cruz Control 179

Hong Kong Karaoke 181

Lima Mist 182

Lokum at the Bazaar 184

Mumbai City 187

Colonel Mustard in the Library with a Dagger 188

Good Year in Ghana 190

Brazilectro 191

Last Flight from Munich 192

Miles Davis in Byblos 193

Sevan Springs Eternal 195

Southeast Asia is known for lots of sweet drinks. And while Thai iced tea is no exception, it does offer some balance with the chewy little tannins from a super-rich brew of Ceylon tea leaves. We've created a cocktail that furthers the balance between some tart citrus notes and the brash, bitter blend of Scotch and Aperol. It's a dryer, more sophisticated way to enjoy one of Thailand's simplest and most well-known drinks. **SERVES 1**

TIGER'S PURR

1½ ounces blended Scotch, Famous Grouse preferred

1½ ounces Thai Tea Syrup (below)

½ ounce Aperol (substitute Campari)

½ ounce lime juice

SERVE WITH
Char Siu Tempeh (page 22)
Singapore Noodles (page 128)

Pour all of the ingredients into an empty shaker. Fill with ice, close the shaker, and shake hard for 12 seconds. Double-strain into a chilled coupe glass.

THAI TEA SYRUP
½ cup Thai (Ceylon) tea leaves   6 tablespoons maple syrup

1 Bring 1 pint water to a boil in a medium saucepan over high heat. Turn off the heat, add the Thai tea leaves, and steep for 10 minutes.

2 Strain out the leaves, stir in the maple syrup, and cool fully before transferring to an airtight container. Store in the refrigerator for up to 1 week.

MAKES 2 CUPS

This pineapple-coconut drink combines two excellent Mexican beverages, horchata and tepache. Horchata is a lightly sweetened rice drink spiked with cinnamon and often made creamy with coconut milk. Tepache is a fermented pineapple juice often with a touch of brown sugar. Our shortcut version serves up the same flavor in just ten minutes. Of course, we use tequila as our base spirit here, and we highly recommend serving a double in a hollowed-out pineapple for an Insta-vacation! It's also worth noting the virgin version is by far our most popular "refreshment" for the nondrinkers in the crowd! **SERVES 1**

CRUZ CONTROL

1½ ounces silver tequila

1 ounce orange liqueur, Dry Curaçao preferred

½ ounce lime juice

1½ ounces Tepache (below)

1½ ounces Horchata (page 180)

Cocktail umbrella and fruit for garnish

SERVE WITH

Salchipapas (page 44)

Huli Huli Barbecue Seitan Tacos (page 99)

Pour the tequila, orange liqueur, lime juice, tepache, and horchata into an empty shaker. Fill with ice, close the shaker, and shake hard for 12 seconds. Double-strain into a tulip glass filled with fresh ice. Garnish with the cocktail umbrella and fruit.

TEPACHE

1 cup pineapple juice

1 ounce white vinegar

½ cup brown sugar

1 cinnamon stick

3 whole cloves

1 Combine all of the ingredients in a medium saucepan over medium heat. Bring to a boil and cook for about 5 minutes.

2 Simmer for an additional 5 minutes, then remove from the heat and strain carefully. Let cool fully before transferring to an airtight container. Store in the refrigerator for up to 5 days.

MAKES 1 CUP

(recipe continues)

(recipe continued from previous page)

HORCHATA

1 cup long-grain white rice	½ cup sugar
One 13.5-ounce can coconut milk	2 cinnamon sticks
	1 teaspoon vanilla extract

1 Combine all of the ingredients and 2 cups water in a medium saucepan over medium heat. Bring to a boil and cook for about 10 minutes.

2 Reduce the heat to low and simmer for an additional 5 minutes, then remove from the heat and strain carefully. Cool fully before transferring to an airtight container. Store in the refrigerator for up to 3 days.

MAKES 1½ CUPS

We have a thing for miso, but it doesn't stop with savory. The rich umami flavors of miso work brilliantly with caramel and butterscotch, so we created a fun Asian cocktail that pairs some serious sweet and smoky booze with a rich caramel apple–miso syrup. While this definitely registers sweet, it's a strong cocktail that will appeal to a wide audience come flannel shirt and apple-picking season, and the syrup itself is so tasty you might make extra to pour over ice cream or pancakes. **SERVES 1**

HONG KONG KARAOKE

1 ounce dark rum, Zaya
    preferred

1 ounce apple brandy,
    Laird's preferred

½ ounce lemon juice

1 ounce Caramel Apple–Miso
    Syrup (below)

½ ounce Scotch-style whiskey,
    Yamazaki preferred

1 dash angostura bitters

1 lemon peel for garnish

SERVE WITH
Sesame Rice Balls (page 157)

Turnip Cakes with Honshimeji XO
    (page 42)

Pour all of the ingredients except the lemon peel into an empty shaker. Fill with ice, close the shaker, and shake hard for 10 seconds. Double-strain into a coupe glass. Garnish with the lemon peel.

CARAMEL APPLE–MISO SYRUP

3 cups chopped apples, such
    as Honeycrisp

¼ cup black vinegar

¼ cup miso

½ cup sugar

¼ cup minced ginger

1 Combine all of the ingredients and 2 cups water in a medium saucepan and bring to a boil over medium heat. Cook for about 10 minutes. Reduce the heat to low and simmer an additional 5 minutes.

2 Remove from the heat. Strain carefully then allow the liquid to cool fully before transferring to an airtight container to store in the refrigerator for up to 1 week.

MAKES 1½ CUPS

Not only did Peru provide the potato to the rest of the world, it somehow gets away with pairing offbeat flavors together like peanuts with lime or olives with cilantro. Once you get a feel for Peruvian cooking, you'll come across its distinct version of a South American fermented corn beverage known as chicha. Our quick version of chicha pairs beautifully with pisco (a light brandy unique to Peru) for a clean, crisp cocktail, one that drinks great as an aperitif with salty snacks. In fact, popped corn makes for a very memorable, edible garnish! **SERVES 1**

LIMA MIST

1 ounce pisco (substitute clear brandy)

4 ounces Chicha (opposite)

¼ ounce lime juice

2 dashes orange flower water (or orange bitters)

Popcorn for garnish

SERVE WITH
Peruvian Fries (page 79)

Palmito with Malagueta Pepper Sauce (page 15)

Pour all of the ingredients except the popcorn into an empty shaker. Fill with ice, close the shaker, and shake hard for 10 seconds. Double-strain into a large rocks glass filled with fresh ice. Insert a straw and garnish with popcorn.

CHICHA

2 cups fresh corn kernels   ½ cup chopped pineapple

½ cup sugar   1 stick cinnamon

½ cup chopped apple   3 whole cloves

1 Combine the corn kernels in a blender with 1½ cups water and blend until smooth. Then strain into a medium sauce pot.

2 Add the remaining ingredients and heat on medium for about 10 minutes or until the fruit has softened and the liquid is reduced by one-quarter.

3 Remove from the heat and cool for about 10 minutes before carefully straining out the solids, pressing the fruits to release any remaining juice.

4 Allow to cool fully before transferring to an airtight container and storing in the refrigerator until ready to use (for up to 5 days).

MAKES 3 CUPS

The Lokum is perhaps the most successful example of our mission to celebrate street food cocktails from around the world. Here we have created a fusion of Turkish coffee with jaleb, a rich fruit juice drink found throughout the Middle East, typically enhanced with some rose water, pomegranate molasses, and pine nuts. Our combination of smoky, bitter tones along with rich fruits and molasses is a little reminiscent of barbecue, so we went ahead and shook it with a little American bourbon. Served in a porcelain New York deli cup, this is a great, boozy cocktail that works well with savory food or at the end of your meal as a coffee/dessert combo. **SERVES 1**

LOKUM AT THE BAZAAR

2 ounces bourbon, Buffalo Trace preferred

1½ ounces Smoked Jaleb (page 186)

1 ounce Turkish Coffee (page 186)

Lemon peel for garnish

SERVE WITH
Savory: Chermoula Hummus with House Pita (page 32)

Sweet: Chocolate-Covered Cherry Alfajores (page 170)

Pour the bourbon, jaleb, and Turkish coffee into an empty shaker. Fill with ice, close the shaker, and shake hard for 12 seconds. Double-strain into a large coffee cup over a large cube of fresh ice. Garnish with a lemon peel.

(recipe continues)

(recipe continued from previous page)

SMOKED JALEB

1 cup chopped dates, pits removed, and smoked for 3 minutes

2 cups pomegranate juice

½ cup sugar

¼ cup molasses

1 cup golden raisins

4 drops rose water

3 ounces sherry vinegar

1 Combine all of the ingredients and 1 cup water in a medium saucepan over medium heat. Bring the mixture to a boil, reduce the heat to low, and simmer for 10 minutes.

2 Strain carefully, pressing on the solids to release all the juice. Let the liquid cool fully before transferring to an airtight container. Store in the refrigerator for up to 1 week.

MAKES 3 CUPS

TURKISH COFFEE

10 cardamom pods, crushed   1 cup espresso powder

1 Pour 2 cups hot water over the cardamom pods in a medium bowl. Let sit for 5 minutes to allow the seeds to perfume the water.

2 Strain out the seeds and add the espresso powder to the water.

3 Cool fully then transfer the coffee to an airtight container. Store in the refrigerator for up to 1 week.

MAKES 3 CUPS

There may be no finer cocktail for warm weather than the classic Pimm's Cup, the wildly garnished blend of lemonade with traditional Pimm's liqueur in all its herbal glory. And while the drink first originated in London, we're taking it to a satellite of the former reaches of the British Empire by introducing a little curry flavor. We also happen to think this is the perfect drink for footballers on MCFB, so it's named for them! Cheers, mate! **SERVES 1**

MUMBAI CITY

1½ ounces Pimm's

1 ounce Curry Syrup (below)

1 ounce Bonal (substitute any off-dry aperitif or dark vermouth such as Cocchi di Torino)

1 ounce lemon juice

Fruit slices, citrus wheels, and herb sprigs for garnish

SERVE WITH
Papadums with Whipped Dal (page 41)

Potato Pakora with Tamarind Sauce (page 36)

Pour the Pimm's, curry syrup, Bonal, and lemon juice into an empty shaker. Fill with ice, close the shaker, and shake hard for 10 seconds. Double-strain into a tulip glass or other footed glass filled with fresh ice. Garnish with fruits and herbs.

CURRY SYRUP

1 cup sugar

½ teaspoon curry powder

2 bay leaves

4 cardamom pods, crushed

1 Combine all of the ingredients and 2 cups water in a medium saucepan over low heat and simmer for 10 minutes.

2 Remove from the heat, strain carefully, and let cool fully before transferring to an airtight container. Store in the refrigerator for up to 1 week.

MAKES 1½ CUPS

Add a bit of the curry syrup to black iced tea for some extra spice.

This cocktail draws inspiration from right here at home in Philadelphia: the soft pretzel. Actually, it's more the staple yellow mustard garnish that we've worked into a daring gin-based cocktail, complete with caramelized onion for a little sweetness! It's basically a take on the classic Corpse Reviver No. 2, but we replace the aromatic absinthe with some zesty mustard. While not for everyone—this is a savory stretch by many counts—it is a signature drink for us, one mustard fans will freak out over—especially when paired with a bready, salty snack! **SERVES 1**

COLONEL MUSTARD IN THE LIBRARY WITH A DAGGER

1 ounce London dry gin, Beefeater preferred

1 ounce Cocchi Americano (substitute Lillet Blanc)

½ ounce lemon juice

1 ounce Mustard Syrup (below)

½ ounce orange liqueur, Cointreau preferred

Pickle for garnish

SERVE WITH
Langos (page 106)
5:00 Szechuan Soft Pretzels (page 30)

Pour all of the ingredients except the pickle into an empty shaker. Fill with ice, close the shaker, and shake hard for 12 seconds. Double-strain into a Collins glass filled with fresh ice. Garnish with a pickle.

MUSTARD SYRUP

½ cup diced white onion

½ cup agave nectar

½ cup Dijon mustard

½ teaspoon caraway seeds

½ teaspoon turmeric

1 ounce sherry vinegar

1 Combine the white onions with ¼ cup water in a medium saucepan over low heat and cook until the onions become translucent, about 20 minutes.

2 Add the remaining ingredients along with ⅓ cup water and simmer for an additional 10 minutes.

3 Remove from the heat, strain carefully, and allow the liquid to cool fully before transferring to an airtight container. Store in the refrigerator for up to 1 week.

MAKES 1½ CUPS

In our tour of street food beverages, we found some inspiration in West Africa. Drawing from chiles, ginger, banana, and other local ingredients, we compiled a spice-forward drink that is off the beaten path but also reminiscent of banana bread. The name comes from the Twi saying Afehyia Pa, *which loosely translates as "May this year go around and meet us again."* **SERVES 1**

GOOD YEAR IN GHANA

1 ounce apple brandy,
    Applejack preferred

½ ounce Ancho Reyes
    chile liqueur

½ ounce walnut liqueur
    (substitute Frangelico
    or Amaretto)

1 ounce Banana Syrup
    (below)

½ ounce lime juice

Lemon peel for garnish

SERVE WITH
Piri Piri Tofu (page 17)

Trumpet Mushroom Shawarma
    (page 109)

Pour all of the ingredients except the lemon peel into an empty shaker. Fill with ice, close the shaker, and shake hard for 12 seconds. Place a large ice cube into a rocks glass and double-strain the contents of the shaker over the ice. Garnish with a lemon peel.

BANANA SYRUP

½ cup brown sugar

½ lime, sliced in wheels

2 cups peeled, sliced ripe
    bananas

1 cinnamon stick

¼ teaspoon turmeric

⅛ teaspoon cardamom

1 teaspoon ginger juice
    (from minced ginger)

1 Bring 2 cups water, the sugar, and lime wheels to a boil in a medium saucepan over high heat and cook for 2 minutes.

2 Add the bananas and cinnamon stick, then reduce the heat to low and simmer until the bananas soften, about 2 minutes. Remove from the heat and cool for 5 minutes before straining out the banana pieces.

3 Add the turmeric and cardamom and let the mixture cool fully. Add the ginger juice and transfer to an airtight container. Keep refrigerated for up to 5 days.

MAKES 1½ CUPS

There's something so attractive, so seductive, so impossibly cool about Brazil. It's like there's a samba soundtrack pulsing through invisible speakers planted in every palm tree. While you're there, you're sure to encounter cachaça, Brazil's take on rum made from fermented sugar juice (instead of fermented molasses). Here we mix it with mezcal, lime juice, and herbs for a tantalizing drink that will have you dancing the forró like a pro in no time! **SERVES 1**

BRAZILECTRO

3 large mint leaves

1½ ounces cachaça

1 ounce Spiced Syrup (below)

½ ounce mezcal, Del Maguey preferred

½ ounce lime juice

Lime wheels and additional mint leaves for garnish

SERVE WITH

Carrot Choripan (page 94)

West Indian Socca with Hearts of Palm and Avocado (page 104)

1 Muddle the mint leaves in the bottom of a shaker with the cachaça. Add the spiced syrup and remaining ingredients except the garnishes into the shaker. Fill with ice, close the shaker, and shake hard for 12 seconds.

2 Double-strain the shaker's contents into a Collins glass filled with fresh ice. Garnish with a lime wheel and fresh mint leaves.

SPICED SYRUP

½ cup sugar

5 whole cloves

1 cinnamon stick

1 tablespoon chopped ginger

1 teaspoon fresh thyme leaves

1 Combine the sugar, 1 cup of water, the cloves, cinnamon, and ginger in a medium saucepan over medium heat, bring to a boil, and cook for 2 minutes.

2 Add the thyme leaves, then reduce heat to low and simmer until the thyme leaves turn dark green, about 2 minutes.

3 Strain the mixture and let cool completely before transferring to an airtight container. Keep refrigerated for up to 5 days.

MAKES 1 CUP

The ultimate holiday cheer experience has to be the Christmas markets in Germany. Go for the glühwein, stay for the pretzels, and don't forget to buy some hand-painted ornaments! If you have wee ones in tow, they'll surely need something to keep warm too, and the Germans have got you covered. Kinderpunsch is traditionally a virgin take on glühwein, packed with all the holiday spice and dried citrus, but without the wine and brandy. We've created our own adult version, which you can enjoy on its own, and it also blends very nicely with a little Scotch. Frohe Weihnachten! **SERVES 1**

LAST FLIGHT FROM MUNICH

1½ ounces blended Scotch, Famous Grouse preferred

1½ ounces orange juice

1 ounce Kinderpunsch (below)

SERVE WITH

Black Garlic Pierogi (page 102)

Pelamushi (page 163)

Pour all of the ingredients into an empty shaker. Fill with ice, close the shaker, and shake hard for 12 seconds. Double-strain into a Collins glass filled with fresh ice.

KINDERPUNSCH

1 bottle merlot (substitute any dry red wine)

5 ounces apple brandy, Laird's preferred

2 cinnamon sticks

15 whole cloves

1 star anise

2 lemons, ends removed and sliced

Peel from 1 grapefruit

¼ cup dried blood orange pieces (substitute dried apple)

2 bay leaves

¼ teaspoon cardamom

1 vanilla bean, split

1½ cups sugar

1 sprig rosemary

1 Combine all of the ingredients in a medium stockpot over medium heat and simmer for 15 minutes.

2 Remove from the heat, strain carefully, then allow the liquid to cool fully before transferring to an airtight container. Store in the refrigerator for up to 2 weeks.

MAKES 5 CUPS

This jazzy cocktail merges a bonded, high-alcohol Kentucky whiskey with a little arak, the delightfully licorice-tasting spirit found in parts of the Middle East. For the syrup, feel free to use whatever orange you prefer, but by cooking the wheels, skins and all, you get a concentrated balance between the floral sweetness of its juice and the bitter notes of its peel. The star anise and vanilla provide the perfect counter for the arak. Then topping with a little sprinkle of coarse salt just before serving makes it all come together and lets the whiskey pop. **SERVES 1**

MILES DAVIS IN BYBLOS

1½ ounces bourbon, Granddad Bonded Whiskey preferred

½ ounce lemon juice

1½ ounces Mandarin Syrup (below)

¼ ounce arak or other licorice liqueur for rinse

Black lava salt for garnish (substitute coarse salt)

SERVE WITH
Za'atar-Grilled Corn with Zhoug (page 86)

Eggplant Sabich (page 117)

1 Pour the bourbon, lemon juice, and syrup into an empty shaker. Fill with ice, close the shaker, and shake hard for 10 seconds.

2 Rinse a rocks glass with the arak, discarding the arak. Double-strain the contents of the shaker into the rinsed glass over a large cube of fresh ice. Sprinkle with the black salt for garnish.

MANDARIN SYRUP

½ cup sugar

½ vanilla bean, split

1 star anise

1 cinnamon stick

5 mandarin oranges, sliced into wheels

1 Bring the sugar and 1 cup water to a boil in a medium saucepan over medium heat. Add the vanilla, star anise, cinnamon, and orange wheels. Cover, reduce the heat to low, and simmer for 20 minutes.

2 Remove from the heat and strain carefully, pressing on the solids to release all the juice. Let the liquid cool fully before transferring to an airtight container. Store in the refrigerator for up to 1 week.

MAKES 2 CUPS

Moroccan cuisine was eye-opening to us: completely aromatic, pulling just a little backbone from sweet spices like cinnamon and clove, packed with savory spices and chiles, and brightened by a fresh herbal punch. While alcoholic libations are somewhat less available there, there are strong beverage traditions that go beyond mint tea. Yogurt-based drinks are hugely popular across North Africa and throughout the Middle East. Often you'll find them sweetened with pomegranate or mango. We developed our own, more akin to tan, the Armenian yogurt drink packed with bright green herbs. Our version also celebrates the spring season with the addition of rhubarb. If you ever find yourself in Armenia, be sure to visit the resort community built up around Lake Sevan. **SERVES 1**

SEVAN SPRINGS ETERNAL

1½ ounces Dolin Génépy (substitute green Chartreuse)

½ ounce Arak (substitute any licorice liquer)

1 ounce Yogurt Base (page 196)

½ ounce lime juice

1 ounce Rhubarb Syrup (page 196)

Rhubarb ribbons for garnish (see tip)

SERVE WITH

Afghani Bolani (page 110)

Harissa Grilled Cauliflower (page 74)

Pour all of the ingredients except the rhubarb ribbons into an empty shaker. Fill with ice, close the shaker, and shake hard for 12 seconds. Pour the shaker's contents directly into a footed tulip glass and garnish with the rhubarb ribbons.

━━━

Run a vegetable peeler down the length of a stalk of rhubarb to turn it into a ribbon. Repeat as desired.

(recipe continues)

(recipe continued from previous page)

YOGURT BASE

½ cup coconut milk	1 teaspoon chopped parsley
2 tablespoons agave syrup	½ cup chopped cucumber, peeled and seeded
1 teaspoon chopped dill	¼ cup vegan yogurt

1 Combine all of the ingredients and ¼ cup water in a blender and blend until smooth.

2 Transfer to an airtight container and store in the refrigerator for up to 3 days.

MAKES 1½ CUPS

RHUBARB SYRUP

1 cup sugar	2 cups chopped rhubarb

1 Combine sugar and 1 cup water in a medium saucepan and bring to a boil over medium heat. Reduce heat to low and simmer while the sugar dissolves, about 3 minutes.

2 Add the rhubarb and simmer for another 5 minutes, to allow the rhubarb to soften.

3 Remove from the heat and strain carefully, mashing the rhubarb to release all its flavor, then let the liquid cool fully before transferring to an airtight container. Store in the refrigerator for up to 5 days.

MAKES 2 CUPS

TRAVEL JOURNAL
COCKTAIL CULTURES

When's the last time you had a Singapore Sling? We were fortunate to sip down two of those delightful cocktails at their birthplace, the iconic Long Bar at the Raffles Hotel in downtown Singapore.

Delightful not so much because they truly please the palate—these days, cocktail culture prescribes bitter amari, perky shrubs, and the freshest of fruits—rather, because of the ritual: sinking into a decades-old time and space, splitting peanut shells and casting them into messy piles on the floor, gazing up at the slow-motion ceiling fans paddling through the thick, tropical air, and raising the curvy glaze of ice-cold strawberry-hued sweetness up to your lips.

Past all the pineapple and maraschino cherry, there's some gin in there somewhere to be sure. But hangover aside, who wouldn't splurge for a sip of history? Legend has it that this particular cocktail was created in an attempt to make alcoholic beverage consumption more socially acceptable for ladies. Kudos.

We seize every opportunity possible to venture to the far corners of the globe to taste the foundations and pillars of modern cocktail culture: caipirinhas in Brazil, piña coladas in Puerto Rico, negronis in Italy . . . We sip beyond the booze and try the local mint or green teas, nut milks, and fruit drinks, all to better understand the broader culinary experience. And at V Street, we design cocktails that are meant to reflect that spirit, carefully pairing the best liqueurs to complement that wide variety of flavors and textures, keeping in mind that we're pairing against the crazy range of street food we serve. From trendier lean and boozy drinks, to thicker, sweet, and colorful cocktails, we love them all, and there's something for everyone!

SAUCES, SPICE BLENDS & MARINADES

XO Sauce 200

Togarashi 201

Ginger Mustard 202

Pickled Red Chile Sauce 203

V Street Sauce 204

Jerk Sauce 206

Piri Piri Marinade 207

Za'atar 208

Latin Spice Blend 210

You might wonder if XO sauce has anything to do with cognac. After all, the French love to label, categorize, and rank things. Well, people in Hong Kong do too, and they've adopted the XO, or Extra Old, labeling system—along with the fancy packaging and everything—for their swanky, spicy fish sauce (often rounded out with some smoky animal products). Some XO sauce bottles are so fancy they could be mistaken for perfume! While we didn't sample much XO in Hong Kong (because of the aforementioned animal products), we did instill our trust in one vegetable tasting menu that promised a "Mushroom" XO. It had a haunting flavor we've been able to re-create Stateside. It's a fantastic complement to all sorts of dishes, but works especially well on simple greens. **MAKES 3½ CUPS**

XO SAUCE

½ cup fermented black bean
   puree

⅓ cup sambal oelek

½ cup black vinegar

1 tablespoon sugar

¼ cup tamari

¼ cup sesame oil

1 tablespoon nori powder
   (see tip)

2 tablespoons chopped ginger

Combine all of the ingredients plus 1½ cups water in a food processor and pulse until just combined, about 20 seconds total. Transfer to an airtight container and store in the refrigerator for up to 2 weeks.

———

If you have nori sheets, cut them into 1-inch pieces and pulverize them with a mortar and pestle or in a clean spice grinder.

THREE OTHER USES FOR NORI POWDER

1. Sprinkle on top of cold salads for a touch of ocean flavor.

2. Throw some in your rice while it's cooking to add nice seaweed flavor.

3. Use as a finish on top of stir-fries.

If your exposure to Japanese cuisine begins and ends with sushi, the obligatory wasabi might lead you to think that spice is big in Japan. But the truth is that there's very little reliance on the chile peppers so prominently featured in other Asian cultures. One significant exception is togarashi. Chock-full of different combinations of sesame seeds, citrus rind, seaweed, and chile, it's a vibrant, peppery condiment you'll see gracing the table of plenty of noodle shops. Its textural and aromatic punch can add a great accent to many Japanese dishes. **MAKES 2 CUPS**

TOGARASHI

½ cup white sesame seeds

½ cup black sesame seeds

⅓ cup red chile flakes

2 sheets nori

1 tablespoon freshly ground black pepper

⅛ cup fine salt

Using a spice grinder or clean coffee grinder, pulse each individual ingredient to a rough powder. Mix all of the ingredients in a small bowl then transfer to an airtight container and store at room temperature for up to 2 weeks.

Chances are you have a packet or two of Chinese mustard sitting in the condiment section of your refrigerator. Well, that was the inspiration for the dipping sauce we serve with our 5:00 Szechuan Soft Pretzels (page 30). As we developed this recipe, we settled on Dijon for the mustard base because it's so naturally thick and creamy. When coupled with the heat from the ginger, the result is a tangy reimagined Chinese mustard that would rock any egg roll!
MAKES 1 CUP

GINGER MUSTARD

1 cup Dijon mustard

½ teaspoon white pepper

1 teaspoon rice wine vinegar

1 teaspoon sugar

2 teaspoons sriracha

1 tablespoon plus 1 teaspoon minced ginger

Whisk together all of the ingredients in a medium bowl until well combined. Transfer to an airtight container and store in the refrigerator for up to 2 weeks.

Super fiery, this Southeast Asian hot sauce would register a 10 for a lot of people. It's based on pickled chile paste, which you can find at nearly any Asian market. While the heat is intense, it's not just heat for heat's sake—it's packed with hauntingly addictive flavor. And it's the perfect accent for rich dishes like Dan Dan Noodles (page 137). **MAKES 1½ CUPS**

PICKLED RED CHILE SAUCE

½ cup pickled chile paste (see tip, below)

2½ tablespoons tamari

2½ tablespoons rice wine vinegar

1 tablespoon sugar

2½ tablespoons sriracha

¼ cup sunflower oil

½ tablespoon tomato paste

Combine all of the ingredients in a food processor with ½ cup water and pulse until well combined. Transfer to an airtight container and store in the refrigerator for up to 2 weeks.

THREE OTHER USES FOR PICKLED CHILE PASTE

1. If you're a spice lover, add it to any Asian soup (½ teaspoon per portion) for a blast of fiery heat.

2. If you're a dragon, drink it.

3. Finish stir-fries with a little at the very end just before serving (don't put it in too early—cooking chiles creates a lot of spicy smoke!).

Nothing says street food quite like hot sauce—that's why we have a few bottles sitting right on our tables at the restaurant. While we try to source rare and interesting brands to experiment with, we also like to offer a signature house version for our guests who like extreme heat. It's constantly evolving based on our culinary inspirations at any given moment, but our most popular incarnation here boasts a near-creamy thickness from the tomato paste and charred pepper. This recipe is a great springboard for improvisation—feel free to add or omit different ingredients to create your own signature style! **MAKES 1¾ CUPS**

V STREET SAUCE

1 cup white vinegar

¾ tablespoon sea salt

1 tablespoon pickled chile paste

1½ tablespoons tomato paste

1 red bell pepper, charred
   (see tip)

1½ garlic cloves, peeled

¼ cup sunflower oil

¼ teaspoon cumin

½ tablespoon cayenne pepper

1 teaspoon black pepper

Combine all of the ingredients in a blender with ¼ cup water and puree on high until smooth. Transfer to an airtight container and store in the refrigerator for up to 2 weeks.

———

Hold the pepper about 4 inches above an open flame on your gas range or grill until it blisters evenly on all sides.

No visit to Jamaica is complete without a quintessential beach barbecue, touristy as it may be. Rice and peas, grilled vegetables, jerk tofu, stews, slaws and salads, every tropical fruit imaginable—all seen through the lens of a rum on the rocks. Throw in the reggae, and this is easily the best memory of your vacation. The most essential element in this barbecue is, obviously, the jerk seasoning. While you'll find all kinds of variations of this sauce or spice rub down in the islands, ours is a deep, dark, and complex combination of sweet tropical spices with a little heat. There are a lot of ingredients, but the prep is easy. This sauce is great for meaty trumpet mushrooms, but creminis and portobello stems make for nice alternatives.

MAKES 2¾ CUPS

JERK SAUCE

½ cup sunflower oil

1 tablespoon brown sugar

1 cup ketchup

1½ tablespoons tamari

1½ cups chopped scallions

1½ tablespoons chopped garlic

1½ tablespoons chopped ginger

½ teaspoon minced Scotch bonnet pepper (substitute jalapeño)

1½ tablespoons fresh thyme leaves

½ cup molasses

1½ teaspoons sea salt

1 tablespoon freshly ground black pepper

¾ tablespoon allspice

⅛ teaspoon ground cloves

¼ teaspoon nutmeg

¾ teaspoon cumin

¼ teaspoon cinnamon

⅓ cup sherry vinegar

Combine all of the ingredients in a blender and blend until smooth. Transfer to an airtight container and store in the refrigerator for up to 2 weeks.

JERK BARBECUE SAUCE

1½ cups Jerk Sauce (above)

1½ cups ketchup

¼ cup plus 2 tablespoons molasses

1 tablespoon agave syrup

1½ tablespoons sriracha

Combine all of the ingredients in a blender and blend until smooth. Transfer to an airtight container and store in the refrigerator for up to 2 weeks.

MAKES 3¼ CUPS

Find a nice Caribbean market (or order online) and get yourself a few jars of piri piri peppers. Also known as malagueta peppers in Brazil, these cherry-red little beauties, packed in a light brine, are loaded with brilliant flavor. This marinade is sensational when grilling our Piri Piri Tofu (page 17), or roasting starchy or hearty vegetables like potatoes or cauliflower. We even use it as a base for an incredibly versatile hot sauce that gives a final shot of high-test tang to wake up any dish. **MAKES 2¼ CUPS**

PIRI PIRI MARINADE

1½ cups sunflower oil

2 tablespoons chopped piri piri peppers (or substitute Calabrian chiles)

6 tablespoons sriracha

2 tablespoons plus 2 teaspoons tamari

2¼ teaspoons preserved lemon

3 tablespoons Old Bay seasoning

1½ tablespoons minced ginger

3 tablespoons minced garlic

Combine all of the ingredients in a food processor and pulse until smooth. Transfer to an airtight container and store in the refrigerator for up to 2 weeks.

PIRI PIRI HOT SAUCE

¼ cup sriracha

¼ cup chopped piri piri peppers (substitute Calabrian chiles)

2 tablespoons white vinegar

1 tablespoon sunflower oil

1 cup Piri Piri Marinade (above)

Combine all of the ingredients plus 2 tablespoons water in a blender and blend until smooth. Transfer to an airtight container and store in the refrigerator for up to 2 weeks.

MAKES 1¾ CUPS

Middle Eastern cuisine, just like its North African and Indian counterparts, is known for aromatic spice blends. And while fresh herbs can add beautiful, bright notes to your cooking, dried or partially dried spice blends can build great layers of flavor. Za'atar is perhaps the best known spice blend, relying on dried oregano, thyme, or other savory herbs, with sesame and sumac as key supporting ingredients. You can customize it however you like; try adding nigella seeds (wild onion seeds) for an earthy, mineral component along with a nice textural crunch. **MAKES ½ CUP**

ZA'ATAR

⅓ cup chopped fresh thyme
  leaves

2 tablespoons sumac

2 tablespoons white sesame
  seeds

2 tablespoons nigella seeds,
  optional

1 teaspoon sea salt

2 teaspoons black peppercorns

Using a spice grinder or clean coffee grinder, pulse each individual ingredient to a rough powder. Mix all of the ingredients in a small bowl then transfer to an airtight container and store in the refrigerator for up to 5 days.

No home kitchen is without its jar of Cajun, Latin, Southwest, blackening, or some kind of bam! spice. There are plenty of great ones out there, and if you have a brand you like, you should stick with it. Just make sure that the first ingredient isn't salt, as that is usually the sign of an inferior product. If you want to go all-out, we like to use (or build upon) this all-purpose blend for many of our Latin or Southwest dishes. **MAKES 2/3 CUP**

LATIN SPICE BLEND

2 tablespoons paprika

2 tablespoons cumin

1 tablespoon granulated garlic

1 tablespoon granulated onion

1 tablespoon salt

1 tablespoon freshly ground
   black pepper

2 teaspoons dried oregano

2 teaspoons dried thyme

1 teaspoon cayenne

2 teaspoons chipotle powder

1 teaspoon coriander

¼ teaspoon ground cloves

Using a spice grinder or clean coffee grinder, pulse each individual ingredient to a rough powder. Mix all of the ingredients in a small bowl, then transfer to an airtight container and store at room temperature for up to 2 weeks.

TRAVEL JOURNAL
FOOD MEMORIES

There are a handful of food memories you create throughout your life when you know, without hesitation, that you'll never taste a better version of what you're eating or drinking: The piping-hot cup of mulled wine at the Christmas markets in Munich, steam dancing up our nostrils teasing us of each baking spice and every chunk of dried citrus peel that steeped in the glühwein. In Buenos Aires, sipping with all our might to get hot mate through a tiny *bombilla*, ignoring any warning from the local *porteños* that it would be far too bitter for us. The single dash of sherry pepper sauce in Bermuda that we knew we had to add to our collection of hot sauces in the refrigerator back home.

We've sipped and tasted a lot of fun things on the road. And so much of the memories has to do with more than just the actual food on your plate. It's the air, it's your view, the language you hear, and the feel of the cup or glass or bowl in your hands. It's all your senses coming together to intoxicate you with a feeling.

These moments are impossible to re-create. Getting out there and experiencing them firsthand is the best way to taste through life. Fresh coconut water, machete-hacked just for you on the streets of Rio, mint tea poured with skill and grandeur in the parlor of an enchanting riad in Marrakech, and sugarcane juice pressed right in the field in Nicaragua, still warm from the beating sun. These are some of our most cherished food memories, and most of them are quite simple, often rugged, and always authentic. We appreciate them for what they were, what we learn from them, and all they continue to inspire us to do in our own kitchen and behind the bar. *Salud!*

...HITO ROBATAYAKI ——————————— 6
shaved daikon, togarashi

PIRI PIRI TOFU ——————————— 7
chermoula potato salad, pickled celery

JERK TRUMPET MUSHROOMS ——————————— 9
sweet potato aioli, escovitch cabbage

MARKET

KUNG PAO GREEN BEANS ——————————— 7
chilled, peanuts, crispy noodle

ZA'ATAR GRILLED CORN ——————————— 6

V STREET

SWEETS

AIS KACANG ————————————————————————
corn custard ice cream, blackberry granita, adzuki,
basil, and pineapple ——————————————— 7

WAFFLE ——————————————————————————
ganache, banana, miso caramel, sriracha peanuts ——— 7

TODAYS SOFT SERVE ——————————————————— 6

AFTER DINNER DRINKS

GREEN TEA POT ——————————————————————
Rishi

AMERICANO ——————————————————————— 4
Philly Fair Trade Roasters

ESPRESSO ———————————————————————— 3
Philly Fair Trade Roasters ——————————— 3

FINAL NOTE

This 777 has been hanging up here forever on our way back from Hong Kong to New York. We have watched all the movies we can watch and drunk as much wine as they would keep pouring for us. It is March of 2016, and the V Street cookbook's now complete and in the hands of our good editors.

What an amazing time it is in the new food culture that plant-based eating is so accepted and even embraced. Many people are waking up to the devastating environmental impact of cattle farming, many are seeing slaughterhouse hidden videos and realizing just how barbaric and inhumane the process of getting meat on the table is. But most people I see are realizing that they are getting older and that staying healthy is becoming more and more appealing to them. Some are prescribed cholesterol medicine because animal products are taking a toll on their bodies. Some people are out of shape and getting worse. They go vegan for a month and are astonished at their weight loss, clear skin and eyes, and newfound energy levels. But most of all, folks are seeing that they really didn't have to sacrifice much in flavor or satisfaction to eat well, live well, and feel well.

This is why V Street has been such an amazing experience for us. From the moment we accept our first morning delivery to the last ticket printing out in the kitchen at night, we are constantly seeking new ways to translate our culinary adventures into exciting and memorable dining experiences. It's a revelation to discover dishes we have never heard of before and to create versions of them for our guests.

We are about moving forward and focusing on the food and that flavor is about good cooking—not about animal meat. It has been amazing to witness chefs in Philadelphia and all over the United States take giant steps toward incorporating more vegetables and vegan dishes into their menus. This truly didn't exist even ten years ago. We consider ourselves lucky to be seen as examples of what is defining the current trends.

As plant-based eating catches on, we find ourselves asked to step onto podiums more and more. We are increasingly asked not just to do a cooking demo, but to speak about what we are doing and why. It's an easy speech for us, often unrehearsed and from the heart. We both got into this for ethical reasons. We are in love with food but perplexed as to why the modern culinary experience is still focused around animal meat.

It drives us, inspires us, and keeps our life spicy. We truly hope you found some inspiration and excitement of your own on the streets of this book or at one of the seats while dining with us at V Street. We hope our "food first" message hits home on every level for you, and that by embracing a plant-based mind-set, whether you are dabbling or diving in headfirst, you are feeling great about it.

UNIVERSAL CONVERSION CHART

OVEN TEMPERATURE EQUIVALENTS

250°F = 120°C

275°F = 135°C

300°F = 150°C

325°F = 160°C

350°F = 180°C

375°F = 190°C

400°F = 200°C

425°F = 220°C

450°F = 230°C

475°F = 240°C

500°F = 260°C

MEASUREMENT EQUIVALENTS
Measurements should always be level unless directed otherwise.

1/8 teaspoon = 0.5 mL

1/4 teaspoon = 1 mL

1/2 teaspoon = 2 mL

1 teaspoon = 5 mL

1 tablespoon = 3 teaspoons = 1/2 fluid ounce = 15 mL

2 tablespoons = 1/8 cup = 1 fluid ounce = 30 mL

4 tablespoons = 1/4 cup = 2 fluid ounces = 60 mL

5 1/3 tablespoons = 1/3 cup = 3 fluid ounces = 80 mL

8 tablespoons = 1/2 cup = 4 fluid ounces = 120 mL

10 2/3 tablespoons = 2/3 cup = 5 fluid ounces = 160 mL

12 tablespoons = 3/4 cup = 6 fluid ounces = 180 mL

16 tablespoons = 1 cup = 8 fluid ounces = 240 mL

ACKNOWLEDGMENTS

Books are a tough business, and cookbooks are especially tough for active chefs. We are fortunate to have incredible people at both restaurants who share our passion and make a project like this possible. Thanks to the team at V Street, especially Lauren and Eric, but also Sam, Lindsey, Gloria, Julieanne, Logan, Rob, and Martin in the BOH. Lauren, you are the glue that keeps us together and the clipboard that keeps us safe and organized. Eric, your palate and perspective are invaluable. Thank you, Ashley, Nina Rose, Keren, and Dre for leading our fantastic FOH team. Steven, Eva, Sadie, Willa, Chris, James, Becca, Derek, Andrea, Randell, Francois, Case, Michelle, and Jordan—you're the best! It's a pleasure to show up for work each day because of your collective happiness, dedication, and talent. At Vedge, thanks to everyone who has helped spread the word about V Street while continuing to keep Vedge at the top of its game: Val and Andrew leading in the kitchen along with David, Elpidio, Greg, Andell, Brandon, and of course Maranda. Plus the entire FOH crew, you're a fantastic group, and you do a great job spreading the word about all the pots we have on the fire!

None of this would be possible without our team at William Morrow. Thank you, Cara Bedick, for being the brainchild of this whole project. Ashley Tucker—your design is brilliant. Kara Zauberman, thank you for your art log finesse and general assistance. Shelby Peak, thanks for keeping us on schedule. And a big thanks to Kaitlyn Kennedy, Emily Homonoff, and Katherine Turro, who have done such a great job bragging about this book and getting the word out!

Thank you, Yoni Nimrod, for your fantastic photography. Not only was it a pleasure working with you, but you nailed the mood and feel we wanted to capture for this book.

To our family and friends who have supported us and encouraged us over the years—thank you from the bottom of our hearts. Mary Jane, Dotsy and Mike, Suzanne and Rob, Rue and Kerry, Ethan, Zara and Eli, Ryan and Khadija—you're all there when we need you, from babysitting to professional advice to drinks, we couldn't do any of this without you.

And Rio—thank you for being our traveling companion on life's journey, from the chaotic hawker stations in Singapore to simple Sunday dinners at our dining room table. You help us continue to see the world with fresh, youthful eyes and an open mind, and you inspire us every day to be stronger, more dedicated, and more creative. Thank you for respecting and taking pride in what we do.

Finally, to each and every guest who grabs a seat at V Street—whether you're a devout Vedge fan carried over from the Horizons days or someone popping in for the first time to see what all the fuss is about with those tempeh tacos—we thank you. We are happy to have put forth another example of vegetable cooking, and we're fortunate to have such a gracious and enthusiastic clientele. We'll keep trying to up our game and keep things exciting! And we look forward to what's next . . .

INDEX

Page numbers in italics indicate photos

5:00 Szechuan Soft Pretzels, 30, 31

Achiote-Marinated Black Beans, 45
Afghani cuisine
    Bolani, 110–11
African cuisine. *See* North African cuisine; West African cuisine
Ais Kacang with Sweet Corn Ice Cream, Blackberry, *152,* 153–55
aji amarillo paste, 80
Alfajores, Chocolate-Covered Cherry, 170–72
Arancini, Sweet Potato, 159–61, *160*
Argentinian cuisine
    Carrot Choripan, 94–96, *95*
    Chocolate-Covered Cherry Alfajores, 170–72
Avocado, West Indian Socca with Hearts of Palm and, 104–05

banana(s)
    Ice Cream, Chocolate-

Peanut Butter Waffles with Curry and, 166–69, *168*
    Syrup, 190
Barbecue Sauce, Jerk, 206
basil seeds, 154
Bean Bhajji, 66
beets
    Langos, 106–08, *107*
Black Beans, Achiote-Marinated, 45
black garlic, 103
    Pierogi, 102–03
black vinegar, 10, 126
    Grilled Sweet Potatoes with, 81
blackberry(ies)
    Ais Kacang with Sweet Corn Ice Cream, *152,* 153–55
    Granita, 154
Blackened Tofu Salad, 52
Bocadillos, 97
Bowls
    Chana Stew, Spicy, 131
    Dan Dan Noodles with Shiitake Mushrooms, *136,* 137–38
    Phat Udon, 134–35
    Ramen, V Street, 132, *133*

Shiitake Dashi with Charred Broccoli, 130
    Singapore Noodles, 128–29
    Soondubu Jjigae, *124,* 125
    Spicy Sesame Noodles, Chilled, *126,* 127
Brazilectro (cocktail), 191
Brazilian cuisine, 121
    Brazilectro (cocktail), 191
    Palmito with Malagueta Pepper Sauce, 15
    Spiced Syrup, 191
bread
    Afghani Bolani, 110–11
    Doubles Bara, 114–15
    House Pita, Chermoula Hummus with, 32–33
    Soft Pretzels, 5:00 Szechuan, 30, *31*
Broccoli, Shiitake Dashi with Charred, 130
Bulgogi, Mushroom, 75

cabbage
    Escoveitch, 63
    Kimchi, V Street, *84,* 85
    Soondubu Jjigae, *124,* 125
Caramel Apple-Miso Syrup, 181

Caramel Corn, Togarashi, 144
Cardamom Puffed Rice Treats,
    Lemongrass Ice Cream
    with, 150–51
Caribbean cuisine. *See also*
    French Caribbean cuisine
    buying ingredients for, 8
    Chana Stew, Spicy, 131
    Doubles Bara Bread, 114–15
    Escoveitch Cabbage, 63
    Jerk Barbecue Sauce, 206
    Jerk Sauce, 206
    Jerk Sweet Potato Salad,
    58, *59*
    Jerk Trumpet Mushrooms,
    20, *21*
    Jerk-Spiced Cashews, 46,
    47
carrot(s)
    Asado, 70, *71*
    Choripan, 94–96, *95*
Cashews, Jerk-Spiced, 46, *47*
cauliflower
    Cauliflower 65, *72*, 73
    Harissa-Grilled, 74
    Salad, Malaysian, 53
Chaat Salad, Spicy, 56, *57*
Chana Stew, Spicy, 131
Char Siu Tempeh, 22
Chermoula Hummus with
    House Pita, 32–33
Cherries, Sour, 149, *149*
Chicha, 183
chickpea flour, 10
chickpeas
    Chana Stew, Spicy, 131
    with Mint Chutney, 62
Chinese cuisine
    5:00 Szechuan Soft
    Pretzels, 30, *31*
    Char Siu Tempeh, 22
    Chòu Dòufu, 26

Dan Dan Noodles with
    Shiitake Mushrooms, *136*,
    137–38
Ginger Mustard, 202
Hoisin-Glazed Seitan
    Skewers, 23
Kung Pao String Beans, 76,
    77
Scallion Pancakes with
    Citrus Ponzu, 38–39
Sweet Potatoes with Black
    Vinegar, Grilled, 81
Turnip Cakes with
    Honshimeji XO, 42–43,
    43
XO Sauce, 200
Chocolate-Covered Cherry
    Alfajores, 170–72
Chocolate-Peanut Butter
    Waffles with Curry-
    Banana Ice Cream,
    166–69, *168*
Chòu Dòufu, 26
Churro Ice Cream Sandwich,
    142–43, *143*
Citrus Ponzu, Scallion
    Pancakes with, 38–39
Cobb Salad, Mexican, *64*, 65
Cocktails
    around the world, 197
    Brazilectro, 191
    Colonel Mustard in the
    Library with a Dagger,
    188, *189*
    Cruz Control, *178*, 179–80
    Good Year in Ghana, 190
    Hong Kong Karaoke, 181
    Kinderpunsch, 192
    Last Flight from Munich, 192
    Lima Mist, 182–83
    Lokum at the Bazaar,
    184–86, *185*

Miles Davis in Byblos, 193
Mumbai City, 187
Seven Springs Eternal, *194*,
    195–96
Tiger's Purr, 176, *177*
coconut
    Torrejas with Guava Butter,
    164–65
    Whipped Cream, 146
coconut milk, 10
Colonel Mustard in the Library
    with a Dagger (cocktail),
    188, *189*
corn
    Ice Cream, Blackberry Ais
    Kacang with Sweet, *152*,
    153–55
    in Quebec City, 49
    with Zhoug, Za'atar-Grilled,
    86, *87*
Crema, Green Chile, 45
Cruz Control (cocktail), *178*,
    179–80
cumin, 10
Curry
    -Banana Ice Cream,
    Chocolate-Peanut Butter
    Waffles with, 166–69, *168*
    Syrup, 187
curry powder, 10

Dal, Papadums with Whipped,
    40, 41
Dan Dan Noodles with
    Shiitake Mushrooms, *136*,
    137–38
Dijon mustard, 10
Doubles Bara Bread, 114–15

eggplant(s)
    Israeli Grilled, 14
    Sabich, *116*, 117

Escoveitch Cabbage, 63

ethnic markets, shopping in
  Caribbean, 8
  Indian, 6
  Japanese, 7
  Korean, 7
  Mexican, 6
  Middle Eastern, 9
  Vietnamese and Thai, 8

Filipino cuisine
  Halo Halo with Sweet
    Potato Ice Cream,
    145–47
five-spice powder, 10
food memories, 211
French Canadian cuisine,
  49
French Caribbean cuisine.
  See also Caribbean
  cuisine
  West Indian Socca with
    Hearts of Palm and
    Avocado, 104–05
Fried Pickles with Spicy
  Ketchup, 34–35

Georgian cuisine
  Pelamushi, *162*, 163
German cuisine
  Kinderpunsch, 192
  Last Flight from Munich
    (cocktail), 192
Ginger Mustard, 202
gochugaru, 10
Good Year in Ghana (cocktail),
  190
granita
  Blackberry, 154
  Orange, 145–46
grape juice
  Pelamushi, *162*, 163

green beans
  Bean Bhajji, 66
  Kung Pao String Beans,
    76, 77
Green Chile Crema, 45
greens
  Market Greens with Pickled
    Turnips, *88*, 89–90
Guava Butter, Coconut
  Torrejas with, 164–65
guava paste, 165

Halo Halo with Sweet Potato
  Ice Cream, 145–47
Halva Ice Cream with Sour
  Cherries, 148–49,
  149
Harissa-Grilled Cauliflower,
  74
Hawaiian cuisine
  Hearts of Palm Slaw, 55
  Huli Huli Barbecue Seitan
    Tacos, *98*, 99–100
  Lomi Tomato Salad, 55
hearts of palm
  Palmito with Malagueta
    Pepper Sauce, 15
  Slaw, 55
  West Indian Socca with
    Avocado and, 104–05
Hoisin-Glazed Seitan Skewers,
  23
Hong Kong cuisine
  Chopped Salad, 60, *61*
  Karaoke (cocktail), 181
  Turnip Cakes with
    Honshimeji XO, 42–43,
    43
  XO Sauce, 200
Honshimeji XO, Turnip Cakes
  with, 42–43, *43*
Horchata, 180

hot sauce
  Piri Piri, 207
  V Street Sauce, 204, *205*
Huli Huli Barbecue Seitan
  Tacos, *98*, 99–100
Hungarian cuisine
  Langos, 106–08, *107*

ice cream
  Curry-Banana, *168*, 169
  Halva, Sour Cherries with,
    148–49, *149*
  Lemongrass, Cardamom
    Puffed Rice Treats with,
    150–51
  Sandwich, Churro, 142–43,
    143
  Sweet Corn, 155, *155*
  Sweet Potato, Halo Halo
    with, 145–47
Indian cuisine
  Bean Bhajji, 66
  buying ingredients for, 6
  Cauliflower 65, *72*, 73
  Chaat Salad, Spicy, 56,
    57
  Chickpeas with Mint
    Chutney, 62
  Curry Syrup, 187
  Mumbai City (cocktail),
    187
  Papadums with Whipped
    Dal, *40*, 41
  Poha Rice, Scrambled,
    112–13
  Potato Pakora with
    Tamarind Sauce, 36,
    37
  Tandoor Zucchini, *18*, 19
Israeli Grilled Eggplant, 14
Italian cuisine, 173. *See also*
  Sicilian cuisine

Jaleb, Smoked, 186
Japanese cuisine, 139
    buying ingredients for, 7
    Citrus Ponzu, Scallion
        Pancakes with, 38–39
    Phat Udon, 134–35
    Ramen, V Street, 132, *133*
    Shishito Robatayaki, *24*, 25
    Togarashi, 201
Jerk
    -Spiced Cashews, 46, *47*
    Barbecue Sauce, 206
    Sauce, 206
    Sweet Potato Salad, 58, *59*
    Trumpet Mushrooms, 20,
        21

Kimchi, V Street, *84*, 85
Kinderpunsch, 192
kombu, 10
Korean cuisine
    buying ingredients for, 7
    Fried Tempeh Tacos, 101
    Kimchi, V Street, *84*, 85
    Mushroom Bulgogi, 75
    Soondubu Jjigae, *124*, 125
Kumquat Marmalade, 151
Kung Pao String Beans, 76,
    77

Langos, 106–08, *107*
Last Flight from Munich
    (cocktail), 192
Latin American cuisine
    Achiote-Marinated Black
        Beans, 45
    Carrot Asado, 70, *71*
    Coconut Torrejas with
        Guava Butter, 164–65
    Green Chile Crema, 45
    Salchipapas, 44–45
    Spice Blend, 210

Lemongrass Ice Cream with
    Cardamom Puffed Rice
    Treats, 150–51
Lima Mist (cocktail), 182–83
Lokum at the Bazaar (cocktail),
    184–86, *185*
Lomi Tomato Salad, 55

Malagueta Pepper Sauce,
    Palmito with, 15
Malaysian cuisine
    Blackberry Ais Kacang with
        Sweet Corn Ice Cream,
        152, 153–55
    Cauliflower Salad, 53
Mandarin Syrup, 193
Marinade(s)
    Piri Piri, 207
Market
    Carrot Asado, 70, *71*
    Cauliflower 65, *72*, 73
    Greens with Pickled Turnips,
        88, 89–90
    Harissa-Grilled Cauliflower,
        74
    Kimchi, V Street, *84*, 85
    Kung Pao String Beans,
        76, *77*
    Mushroom Bulgogi, 75
    Peruvian Fries, *78*, 79–80
    Sweet Potatoes with Black
        Vinegar, Grilled, 81
    Togarashi Home Fries, 82,
        83
    Za'atar-Grilled Corn with
        Zhoug, 86, *87*
Marmalade, Kumquat, 151
Marrakech, 67
Mexican cuisine
    Blackened Tofu Salad, 52
    buying ingredients for, 6
    Cobb Salad, *64*, 65

Cruz Control (cocktail), *178*,
    179–80
Horchata, 180
Tepache, 179
Middle Eastern cuisine
    buying ingredients for, 9
    Chermoula Hummus with
        House Pita, 32–33
    Eggplant Sabich, *116*, 117
    Israeli Grilled Eggplant, 14
    Jaleb, Smoked, 186
    Lokum at the Bazaar
        (cocktail), 184–86, *185*
    Miles Davis in Byblos
        (cocktail), 193
    Trumpet Mushroom
        Shawarma, 109
    Turkish Coffee, 186
    Za'atar, 208, *209*
    Za'atar-Grilled Corn with
        Zhoug, 86, *87*
Miles Davis in Byblos
    (cocktail), 193
Mint Chutney, Chickpeas
    with, 62
molasses, 10
Moroccan cuisine, 67
    Harissa-Grilled Cauliflower,
        74
    Olive Salad, 54
    Seven Springs Eternal
        (cocktail), *194*, 195–96
Mumbai City (cocktail), 187
mushroom(s)
    Bulgogi, 75
    Dan Dan Noodles with
        Shiitake Mushrooms, *136*,
        137–38
    Jerk Trumpet Mushrooms,
        20, *21*
    Pho French Dip, *118*,
        119–20

mushroom(s) (continued)
    Shiitake Dashi with Charred
        Broccoli, 130
    Trumpet Mushroom
        Shawarma, 109
mustard powder, 56
Mustard, Ginger, 202

noodles
    Dan Dan Noodles with
        Shiitake Mushrooms, *136,*
        137–38
    Phat Udon, 134–35
    Ramen, V Street, 132, *133*
    Sesame, Chilled Spicy, *126,*
        127
    Singapore, 128–29
nori powder, 200
North African cuisine
    Chermoula Hummus with
        House Pita, 32–33
nuts
    Cashews, Jerk-Spiced, 46,
        47
    Peanuts, Sriracha, 48

Olive Salad, Moroccan, 54
Orange Granita, 145–46

Pakora with Tamarind Sauce,
    36, *37*
Palmito with Malagueta
    Pepper Sauce, 15
pantry staples, 10–11
Papadums with Whipped Dal,
    40, 41
Pelamushi, *162,* 163
peppers
    Shishito Robatayaki, *24,* 25
Peruvian cuisine
    Chicha, 183
    Fries, *78,* 79–80

Lima Mist (cocktail),
    182–83
Phat Udon, 134–35
Pho Broth, 120
Pho French Dip, *118,* 119–20
pickled chile paste, 203
Pickled Red Chile Sauce, 203
Pierogi, Black Garlic, 102–03
Piri Piri
    Hot Sauce, 207
    Marinade, 207
    Tofu, *16,* 17
Plates
    Afghani Bolani, 110–11
    Black Garlic Pierogi,
        102–03
    Bocadillos, 97
    Carrot Choripan, 94–96,
        95
    Eggplant Sabich, *116,* 117
    Huli Huli Barbecue Seitan
        Tacos, *98,* 99–100
    Korean Fried Tempeh Tacos,
        101
    Langos, 106–08, *107*
    Pho French Dip, *118,*
        119–20
    Poha Rice, Scrambled,
        112–13
    Trumpet Mushroom
        Shawarma, 109
    West Indian Socca with
        Hearts of Palm and
        Avocado, 104–05
Poha Rice, Scrambled, 112–13
popcorn
    Togarashi Caramel Corn,
        144
Portuguese cuisine, 27
    Piri Piri Hot Sauce, 207
    Piri Piri Marinade, 207
    Piri Piri Tofu, *16,* 17

potato(es)
    Bean Bhajji, 66
    Langos, 106–08, *107*
    Pakora with Tamarind
        Sauce, 36, *37*
    Peruvian Fries, *78,* 79–80
    Pierogi, Black Garlic,
        102–03
    Salchipapas, 44–45
    Togarashi Home Fries, 82,
        83
Puffed Rice Treats,
    Lemongrass Ice Cream
    with Cardamom, 150–51
pumpkin
    Afghani Bolani, 110–11

Quebec City, 49

Ramen, V Street, 132, *133*
Red Chile Sauce, Pickled, 203
Rhubarb Syrup, 196
rice
    Arancini, Sweet Potato,
        159–61, *160*
    Balls, Sesame, *156,* 157–58
    Scrambled Poha, 112–13
rice wine vinegar, 10
Roman pastry shops, 173

Salads & Slaws
    Bean Bhajji, 66
    Blackened Tofu Salad, 52
    Chickpeas with Mint
        Chutney, 62
    Escoveitch Cabbage, 63
    Hearts of Palm Slaw, 55
    Hong Kong Chopped Salad,
        60, *61*
    Jerk Sweet Potato Salad,
        58, *59*
    Lomi Tomato Salad, 55

Malaysian Cauliflower Salad, 53

Mexican Cobb, *64*, 65

Moroccan Olive Salad, 54

Spicy Chaat Salad, 56, *57*

Salchipapas, 44–45

sambal oelek, 11, 53

Sauce(s)

Citrus Ponzu, Scallion Pancakes with, 38–39

Dan Dan, 138

Ginger Mustard, 202

Green Chile Crema, 45

Honshimeji XO, Turnip Cakes with, 42–43, *43*

Jerk, 206

Jerk Barbecue, 206

Mint Chutney, Chickpeas with, 62

Pickled Red Chile, 203

Piri Piri Hot, 207

Singapore, 129

Spicy Ketchup, Fried Pickles with, 34–35

Tamarind, Potato Pakora with, 36, *37*

V Street, 204, *205*

XO, 200

Zhoug, Za'atar-Grilled Corn with, 86, *87*

seitan

Skewers, Hoisin-Glazed, 23

Tacos, Huli Huli Barbecue, *98*, 99–100

sesame

Noodles, Chilled Spicy, *126*, 127

Rice Balls, *156*, 157–58

sesame oil, 11

Seven Springs Eternal (cocktail), *194*, 195–96

Shawarma, Trumpet Mushroom, 109

sherry vinegar, 11

Shiitake Dashi with Charred Broccoli, 130

Shishito Robatayaki, *24*, 25

shopping in ethnic markets, 5–9

Sicilian cuisine. *See also* Italian cuisine

Sweet Potato Arancini, 159–61, *160*

Singaporean cuisine

cocktails, 197

Noodles, 128–29

Sauce, 129

Snacks

5:00 Szechuan Soft Pretzels, 30, *31*

Chermoula Hummus with House Pita, 32–33

Fried Pickles with Spicy Ketchup, 34–35

Jerk-Spiced Cashews, 46, *47*

Papadums with Whipped Dal, *40*, 41

Potato Pakora with Tamarind Sauce, 36, *37*

Salchipapas, 44–45

Scallion Pancakes with Citrus Ponzu, 38–39

Sriracha Peanuts, 48

Turnip Cakes with Honshimeji XO, 42–43, *43*

Soft Pretzels, 5:00 Szechuan, 30, *31*

Soondubu Jjigae, *124*, 125

Sour Cherries, 149, *149*

South American cuisine, 121

Brazilectro (cocktail), 191

Carrot Choripan, 94–96, *95*

Palmito with Malagueta Pepper Sauce, 15

Peruvian Fries, *78*, 79–80

Spiced Syrup, 191

Southeast Asian cuisine

Pickled Red Chile Sauce, 203

Southern cuisine

Fried Pickles with Spicy Ketchup, 34–35

Spanish cuisine

Bocadillos, 97

Spice Blends

Jerk Spice, 46

Latin, 210

Togarashi, 201

Za'atar, 208, *209*

Spiced Syrup, 191

Spicy Ketchup, Fried Pickles with, 34–35

sriracha, 11

Sriracha Peanuts, 48

star anise, 120

Stew, Spicy Chana, 131

Sticks

Char Siu Tempeh, 22

Chòu Dòufu, 26

Hoisin-Glazed Seitan Skewers, 23

Israeli Grilled Eggplant, 14

Jerk Trumpet Mushrooms, 20, *21*

Palmito with Malagueta Pepper Sauce, 15

Piri Piri Tofu, *16*, 17

Shishito Robatayaki, *24*, 25

Tandoor Zucchini, *18*, 19

string beans

Bean Bhajji, 66

Kung Pao String Beans, 76, *77*

sunflower oil, 11

sweet potato(es)
  Arancini, 159–61, *160*
  Ice Cream, Halo Halo with, 145–47
  Salad, Jerk, 58, *59*
  with Black Vinegar, Grilled, 81
Sweets
  Blackberry Ais Kacang with Sweet Corn Ice Cream, *152*, 153–55
  Blackberry Granita, 154
  Chocolate-Covered Cherry Alfajores, 170–72
  Chocolate-Peanut Butter Waffles with Curry-Banana Ice Cream, 166–69, *168*
  Churro Ice Cream Sandwich, 142–43, *143*
  Coconut Torrejas with Guava Butter, 164–65
  Coconut Whipped Cream, 146
  Halo Halo with Sweet Potato Ice Cream, 145–47
  Halva Ice Cream with Sour Cherries, 148–49, *149*
  Kumquat Marmalade, 151
  Lemongrass Ice Cream with Cardamom Puffed Rice Treats, 150–51
  Orange Granita, 145–46
  Pelamushi, *162*, 163
  Sesame Rice Balls, *156*, 157–58
  Sweet Potato Arancini, 159–61, *160*
  Togarashi Caramel Corn, 144

tacos
  Huli Huli Barbecue Seitan, *98*, 99–100
  Korean Fried Tempeh, 101
tamari, 11
tamarind paste, 37
Tamarind Sauce, Potato Pakora with, 36, *37*
Tandoor Zucchini, *18*, 19
tempeh
  Char Siu, 22
  Tacos, Korean Fried, 101
Tepache, 179
Thai cuisine
  buying ingredients for, 8
  Tea Syrup, 176
  Tiger's Purr (cocktail), 176, *177*
Thai Tea Syrup, 176
Tiger's Purr (cocktail), 176, *177*
tofu
  around the world, 91
  Chòu Dòufu, 26
  Piri Piri, *16*, 17
  Poha Rice, Scrambled, 112–13
  Salad, Blackened, 52
  Soondubu Jjigae, *124*, 125
Togarashi, 201
  Caramel Corn, 144
  Home Fries, 82, *83*
Tokyo noodle bars, 139
Tomato Salad, Lomi, 55
Torrejas with Guava Butter, Coconut, 164–65
travel and food memories, 211
trumpet mushroom(s)
  Jerk, 20, *21*
  Shawarma, 109
Turkish Coffee, 186

turnip(s)
  Cakes with Honshimeji XO, 42–43, *43*
  Market Greens with Pickled, *88*, 89–90

V Street
  Kimchi, *84*, 85
  Ramen, 132, *133*
  Sauce, 204, *205*
vegan butter, 11
vegan mayo, 11
Vietnamese cuisine
  buying ingredients for, 8
  Pho Broth, 120
  Pho French Dip, *118*, 119–20

Waffles with Curry-Banana Ice Cream, Chocolate-Peanut Butter, 166–69, *168*
West African cuisine
  Banana Syrup, 190
  Good Year in Ghana (cocktail), 190
West Indian Socca with Hearts of Palm and Avocado, 104–05
Whipped Cream, Coconut, 146
white pepper, 11

XO Sauce, 200

Yogurt Base, 196

Za'atar, 208, *209*
  -Grilled Corn with Zhoug, 86, *87*
Zucchini, Tandoor, *18*, 19

ABOUT THE AUTHORS

Rich Landau and **Kate Jacoby** are the husband-and-wife chefs and owners of Vedge, a vegetable restaurant that opened in 2011 to rave reviews from diners and critics alike, and V Street, a street food bar where vegetables remain the center of the dish.

Landau broke onto the vegetable cooking scene in 1994, when he opened his first restaurant, Horizons. As executive chef for both restaurants, he is a James Beard Award Finalist and, together with Jacoby, served the first-ever vegan dinner at the James Beard House. Jacoby is the executive pasty chef for both Vedge and V Street and has also been a James Beard Nominee. She is also a certified sommelier with the Court of Master Sommeliers and oversees the restaurants' beverage programs.

They live in their native Philadelphia with their son Rio.

ABOUT V STREET

V Street is a street food bar by Vedge chef-owners Rich Landau and Kate Jacoby.

The menu is inspired by great ethnic and street foods of the world. Rather than creating anything too literal, V Street uses these great flavors to create a new dining experience full of bold spice and adventurous flavors.

And yeah, it's vegan.